HOW TO START A CLOTHING COMPANY

LEARN BRANDING, BUSINESS, OUTSOURCING, GRAPHIC DESIGN, FABRIC, FASHION LINE APPAREL, SHOPIFY, FASHION, SOCIAL MEDIA, AND INSTAGRAM MARKETING STRATEGY

TABLE OF CONTENTS

INTRODUCTION 1

CHAPTER 1 6
  BEFORE YOU BEGIN: SECURING YOUR BUSINESS LICENSES

CHAPTER 2 17
  BRANDING: IT IS NOT AS HARD AS YOU THINK

CHAPTER 3 25
  THE BEST BUSINESS MODEL FOR YOUR CLOTHING BUSINESS

CHAPTER 4 33
  LAYING THE GROUND WORK: CLOTHING AND FABRIC FUNDAMENTALS

CHAPTER 5 41
  GRAPHIC DESIGN AND CLOTHING DESIGN: WHAT YOU NEED TO KNOW

CHAPTER 6 53
  CREATE YOUR COMPANY'S WEBSITE THE EASY WAY

CHAPTER 7 63
  FINDING YOUR PERFECT MANUFACTURER

CHAPTER 8 74
  SMART MARKETING 101

CHAPTER 9 91
  ORDER FULFILLMENT CRASH COURSE

CHAPTER 10 101
  MONEY, MONEY, MONEY, MONEY

CONCLUSION 109

INTRODUCTION

Congratulations on choosing *How to Start a Clothing Company: Learn Branding, Business, Outsourcing, Graphic Design, Fabric, Fashion Line Apparel, Shopify, Fashion, Social Media, and Instagram Marketing Strategy*, and thank you for doing so.

An unknown wise person once said, 'The dream is free, but the hustle is sold separately." The road to becoming an entrepreneur is not easy. For many who want to embark upon the clothing entrepreneur lifestyle, they have no problem thinking about their lofty goals of fame and fortune. Yet, in order to reach their goals, they have to put in the work, or the hustle. This path is even more difficult if you want to make it in the clothes business. Clothing is one of the most difficult businesses in which to be successful due to the competitive nature of the niche. While it may be difficult to achieve success, is not impossible. Many people have started thriving clothing companies, and these brands are some of our most popular and iconic brands today, such as Gucci, Versace, Michael Kors, and even your favorite brand. These brands did not start off being successful. They built their way to the top from the bottom. If you are interested in starting a clothing company, you too can start and build your way to the top of the success ladder.

This book is all about helping you achieve your dreams to launch your dream clothing company, whether you want to have a local boutique in your town's downtown square or if you want to be an internationally-known, luxurious brand worn by the most famous celebrities. All clothing brands have common pieces that they need to be successful. The most important common denominator between all these brands is the hard work that the founders put in to jumpstart their company's success. Do not take the words 'hard work' lightly. To be successful, you will be required to put in lots of hard work. Hard work means sleepless nights, days with no money, obstacles that you feel like you cannot overcome, even debt and stress. Hard work can mean that your friends and family do not understand why you are staying up at all hours of the night to make your dream come true instead of hanging out with them. Hard work means that you may have to isolate yourself for a time until you meet your business goals. Hard work means that you may be alone. However, the end goal is worth it and the owners of some of the most successful clothing companies will agree.

So why would somebody want to leave the comfortable life of working a regular, stable, nine-to-five job and embark upon the unstable, wild world of owning your own business? There are many reasons. The thrill of being your own boss is the first reason. Many people love to do what they want to do when they want to do it. When you are your own boss, you do not have to worry about others telling you what to do. YOU are the one that gets to tell others what to do, and they HAVE to listen to you. When you are an entrepreneur, you have the joy of being able to take what you see in your mind and make it become reality. There is an unspeakable rush when you see others wearing your creation. Another major reason for becoming a clothing entrepreneur is attractive because you are paid what you are worth. If you were working a traditional job, you would be paid an hourly rate, oftentimes wishing that you were making more money. However, the amount of money you can make from owning your own business is astronomically higher than you can but working for someone else. The work to pay ratio when you are an entrepreneur is definitely better. That work to pay ratio is limitless, especially if your clothing business is successful. When you own your own business, someone does not become rich off of your hard work. When you own your own business, you do not have to dread going to work every day, knowing that someone is living a comfortable lifestyle from your hard work. As a business owner, you, and only you are the beneficiary of all your hard work. You determine what other people make, whether they are employees or freelancers because you are in charge. If you want to cut everyone's pay, you can. If you want to give everyone a raise, you can. You are the boss and what you say GOES. This book will help you begin the journey towards owning your own business and becoming the boss you are destined to be.

For some who already have capital saved up, they are ready to jump head into starting their own clothing empire. For others, they may have to work while building your clothing empire on the side. The great thing about either method is that you are taking action. That's the most important thing to take away from this book. If you do not remember anything else, remember this. The sooner you start, the sooner you will be able to have the clothing business of your dreams. You do not have to know everything up front. You do not have to wait until everything is perfect. Many people waste time biting their fingernails and stressing over what moves to make. Approach your business as a marathon. It is not a sprint. You have to get started in order to reach the end. You also need to be flexible with change because as a business owner, things in the business world change all the time. Know that your business idea and business methods are going to change many times until you get comfortable. The best way to get comfortable is to start.

The following chapters will help you start. They will discuss everything you need to know to start your dream clothing company. In chapter 1, you will learn about the business licenses that you need to begin. You will also learn the best ways to organize your business structure to legally protect yourself and your assets. In Chapter 2, you learn all about branding. We will explore questions that you should ask yourself before you begin in order to have a long successful clothing company career and brand. We get to the fun stuff in chapter 3 where we will discuss how to bring your clothing ideas to life. You will be given different clothing business models to choose from, and you can decide the best route to take. Chapter 4 breaks down the fundamentals of fabric and clothing. It serves as a glossary to help you understand the pros and cons of the types of styles you want to create. Graphic designing and clothing designing will be the subject of chapter 5. Chapter 6 will help you figure out the best design for your website and how to have it created. In chapter 7, the types of manufacturers you can use will be explained. The easy way to use overseas manufacturers will also be explored. In chapter 8, attention will be given to the different marketing tools you can use with a special section on the benefits of social media, especially Instagram. In chapter 9, order fulfillment will be discussed, and the book will end with chapter 10 discussing how to reinvest your profits that you are raking in to further excel your business to the top. You will also learn about getting tax deductions for your business so when it comes time to pay taxes you have a lower amount of taxes to pay.

The information provided can feel overwhelming, but it is important to note that by the time you finish, you will have everything you need to do to start your clothing business. Just take everything step-by-step, and you will be moving towards your goals in no time. Be mindful that there are lots of things that you may have to do on your own. There are lots of things to research. (Remember, it takes hard work.) The more you research in the more you connect with people who are doing what you want to do, the easier your journey will be. Always be open to learning more because you must be adaptable as a business owner if you're going to be successful. There is no way around it. However, if you are determined to succeed, you will be able to overcome any challenges that you may face. Stay positive and keep going. Think of failure as a lesson and turn it into a positive thing. You will only know what works once you fail. So, fail a lot and learn a lot.

There are plenty of books on this subject on the market, thanks again for choosing this one! Every effort was made to ensure it is full of as much useful information as possible, please enjoy!

CHAPTER 1

BEFORE YOU BEGIN: SECURING YOUR BUSINESS LICENSES

Congratulations are in order. You have decided to launch your clothing company. You've decided to take a step that many people are too scared to even try. Before you begin, there are a few things you need to have in place that will form the backbone of your business. When you are in the initial phase of starting your business, you want to make sure that you have all the necessary business paperwork that you need so you will not be subjected to any financial trouble once your business becomes successful. This chapter will walk you through selecting your business name, getting your seller's permit, a wholesale license, and the easiest way to form your business when you are first beginning. These steps are going to require you to use your research skills. You will have to find some information on your own. It may be difficult especially if you have not done it before. However, the good thing is that these steps are free and there are a lot of resources you will be given in this chapter that can help you should you run into any trouble. Let's begin.

The first thing you want to determine before you begin is what your name will be. You can use any type of method to come up with your name. Some people like to use their initials. Others use family names or names that have significance from important events in their life. Have fun! This is your business. However, keep in mind that your name can be a hindrance to people who will want to invest in your business. You want to make sure that the name is professional and attractive enough that lenders will not mind lending to you if necessary. You also do not want to have a profane or offensive name that can prevent you from making sales further along the line. Ultimately you can take whatever route you want but keeping the professionalism in a business name is advised. Once you have your name, you want to make sure that is not trademarked by anyone else. The first thing you can do is to do a simple Google search of the name to see what pops up. You can also check your state's Secretary of State office to check for names of businesses in your state. To do so, Google 'Secretary of State business name search' and the name of your state. You can put your business name in the search bar and see if anything pops up. Then you will want to see if your name is already trademarked. You can visit the United States Patent and Trademark Office online and do a quick search there. If there is another business with your name, do not fret. You still may be able to use the name. If there is not another business name trademarked in your state with the same name, you are free to use the name. If you are concerned about your business's name and want to have all the protection you can get, you may consider trademarking your business' name. It is an additional cost. It is not necessary starting out, but some people like to have that protection. Oftentimes, people like to get started with the least amount necessary and then upgrade as their business makes more money.

After you get you get your business name, then you want to figure out how to structure your business. Small businesses are often times structured differently from larger businesses. However, at any time you can always restructure your business. So do not feel pressured to have it one way. Oftentimes businesses change, so go ahead and get comfortable with constant changes. When deciding how to structure your business, you will want to consider if you want to get started doing business as soon as possible or wait a little bit later to have everything structured a certain way before you begin. The easiest way to structure your business is by setting it up as a sole proprietorship. The sole proprietorship is technically not a legal entity. A sole proprietorship just means that the person who owns the business is responsible for its debt. A sole proprietor uses their own social security number as the business tax ID. A tax ID is important because it helps the government know who to contact about getting taxes when you make money. When you set your business up as a sole proprietorship, if something happens, like someone has an allergic reaction from your clothing and they sue you, you will be responsible for battling the issue in court. Using your own social security for your business means that if your business suffers any financial setback and the business cannot pay from its profits, you will have to use your personal money to pay for the debt.

Some people do not feel comfortable using their own social security number to operate their business, so they use a different method. This method is similar to structuring their business as a sole proprietorship, but they just create a new tax ID for the business. The new tax ID is called an EIN. The EIN stands for Employer Identification Number (EIN), or the Federal Tax Identification Number. It is entirely free to procure. It can take a few weeks, anywhere from 4 to 5 weeks to get your EIN number. Once you get your EIN number, if this is the option you want to take, then you can apply for a seller's permit or a wholesale license. When you have your EIN number, you can still operate your business as a sole proprietor, but instead of using your social security number the business's tax ID will be the EIN number instead. The EIN number also gives you certain advantages that you can use when operating your business that a social security number does not. For example, if you have your EIN number, you are able to hire employees. You are also able to protect yourself from identity theft better. Some people like to structure their business as a use a sole proprietor because of ease of use. You can apply for your EIN, receive it and be good to go. If you are going to run everything on your own in your business, this may be the easiest way to get started.

However, another popular way that people like to use to structure their business is by creating an LLC. LLC means a limited liability company. They like the extra protection that an LLC provides. If you have an LLC, and your business is sued or falls into financial difficulty, you are not obligated to pay the debts from your personal assets. You are also protected from being sued for anything as your business would be responsible, not you the sole proprietor. An LLC can be created online, using sites like Legal Zoom, and it can be created in any state that you would like to give your business better protections. No matter how you structure your business, many people like to use their home address as the place to set up their business. However, this isn't ideal because your information will be made known public and random people, or debt collectors will have access to your information. Identity theft is real, so you want to make sure that you are taking the proper precautions. There is nothing worse than thinking that it will not happen to you and it does. Prevent this from happening. Protect your information. When setting up your business, you may want to consider using a PO Box at your local post office, which is a small yearly fee, or using a virtual office, also a small monthly fee, that allows you use a different address than your regular address. Some people even rent a different house in order to use the house's address, but that is an expensive option. Using a PO Box or virtual office is also helpful if you are trying to create your LLC in a different state. They just get the virtual office in the state that they want to create the LLC in and use the virtual address on the LLCs application. Certain states have better tax benefits for business and are popular to create an LLC in the state.

The top three states at the time of writing are Nevada, Wyoming, or Delaware. These places are typically more business-friendly and have limited income taxes. Delaware is popular because they do not tax out-of-state income. This means that if your business makes money outside of Delaware you won't be taxed for it. Nevada is another popular destination to create an LLC because they do not tax business income, and they have a high level and anonymity in case the feds were to ask questions about your business. Wyoming is another popular place because they do not tax business income as well, and they have a higher level of anonymity than Nevada does. If you wanted to set up your LLC in one of these places, you could. It will be more expensive than a sole proprietorship. Also, the rules for LLCs change constantly depending on the state so you would be responsible for staying up to date on the state's rules. You would just research their rules on the states IRS or Secretary of State's office online. Some people like to start off as a sole proprietorship, and as they make more money, create the LLC. Some LLC's require that you pay a yearly fee. You would have to research to see what applies for that state. Popular places to format your LLC is only by doing it yourself if you feel comfortable finding all the information. Other people like to visit a lawyer's office and get their assistance. This may be expensive, but there are some lawyers that can help you for free if you visit your city's local Chamber of Commerce. They would be able to help you find lawyers who can help you pro bono (free of charge). Other business structures are an S-Corp or C-corp, but these type of business structures are reserved for extremely large companies.

    If you ever wanted to start the business with a friend, you can set it up as a partnership, which is like a sole proprietorship, but it is just two or more people. You can get the EIN for the business or you can even set it up as an LLC. You want to set up your business properly from the beginning to avoid headaches later. If you have the funds, you can probably set up an LLC, but the easiest entry is going to be with the sole proprietorship or a partnership. At the very minimum, try to have an EIN number for your business, because of the added protection, and it is free.

There are also a few more differences you will want to consider when deciding to register your business as a sole proprietorship or an LLC. They are as follows:

- A sole proprietorship is cheaper to begin than an LLC. You must register the LLC in the state that your business is located in. You may have to pay an annual LLC filing fee depending on the state. An LLC also must follow the state's bylaws pertaining to LLC conduct.
- An LLC requires that your business finances and business records are separate from your personal finances and records. This means that you must have a separate banking account for your LLC. This requirement is not necessary for a sole proprietorship but is also advised that you have a separate business account. That way you can keep your finances separate.
- An LLC required that you have a registered agent. A registered agent must live in the state that you are registering your LLC in, and they are responsible for being able to receive all communications regarding your business. Some people like to use a registered agent company for this.

- When you have a sole proprietorship, you are tax as a self-employed person. Whereas when you have an LLC, you can be taxed as a sole proprietor, partnership, or corporation.

When trying to decide how to register your business, you can also consult a lawyer or accountant for further questions. To save costs, try to visit a local law clinic at a university where you can get advice from local law students. They are a valuable resource to use when you are trying to find out legal questions for your business. You can also check out nonprofits in the area to see if they have pro bono lawyers that are willing to do work. There is lots of free legal advice everywhere you go. You just have to find it.

After you have your business structure, you can then apply for a sellers' permit. The seller's permit is important to have because it allows you to sell goods and products as a business. The seller's permit also allows you to collect sales tax for the products that you sell. It is important for you to collect sales tax because you must pay those taxes quarterly to your state government. Lucky for you, a seller's permit is relatively easy to obtain. The place to obtain the seller's permit is going to vary state by state. The seller's permit may even vary city by city if you live in a very large state. How much sales tax you need to collect will also vary state by state. The easiest way to find where you need to get a seller's permit is to Google your city's name and sellers permit. Usually, the first link that opens is going to be the officer that you can go to and purchase your seller's permit.

Most seller's permits come as a temporary permit for selling at temporary events, like flea markets or fairs or pop-ups, or you can get a permanent seller's permit. If you want to make this a long-term business, make sure that you are filling out the application for a long-term seller's permit. Once you get the seller's permit printed off, fill it out. You can either return the seller's permit form by mail or in person. Make sure that you fill out all the information as correctly as possible to avoid any delays in getting your application processed. Another way to find the place where to get your seller's permit is to Google your state's name and 'Board of Equalization'. This will have the different regions of your state and the locations where to get your sales permit. It is important to know where to find their information because they can help you figure out where to find your local agency that can assist further. If you run into any issues, feel free to call the numbers or email them with any questions that you may have. The information they give you is free, and it is funded by taxpayers' dollars already so do not be shy to ask them. The service is already paid for. Another great resource for helping you find any permits you may need will be business.gov. This is a federal website that promotes small businesses in the country. They have other great resources for you to use. As a quick note, how long it takes to get your seller's permit can vary state by state so if you are in a rush, be sure to ask your local agency the processing time so you can make sure that you have everything in place before you begin selling. It is advisable that you do not start selling until you have your sales permit. That way you will not have to worry about any issues regarding your taxes. Another thing is, you will also want to make sure that you have your sales taxes in order too if you are selling items online. You may even be responsible for sales tax on your website dependent on the state where the other person is buying from. When you are applying for your seller's permit, be sure to have the proper rates for sales and use taxes for your state. The attendants at the local agency will be able to help you. This information varies state-by-state, so make sure you have the right information for your state. There are payment software's PayPal or stripe you will use to accept payment from your customers. During tax season they will send you statements regarding your sales.

After you get your seller's permit, you may also need to get your wholesale license. This permit allows you to buy directly from distributors and manufacturers without having to pay retail sales tax so you can resell their products. By buying at a lower rate from a manufacturer or distributor, you will be able to make your price higher and make more profit. However, most of these businesses will not sell to you if you do not have a wholesale license. Depending on your state, the Board of Equalization may combine the seller's permit and the wholesale license so be sure to ask them if you need to get a separate wholesale license when you are applying for your seller's permit.

While you are structuring your business, you will also want to think about the future of your business long-term. This is called thinking about your exit strategy. Will you want to be the CEO of your business until it reaches the highest height? Would you be interested in selling your business in case it is successful and a bigger brand wanted to buy it? Are you committed to seeing your brand become a wealthy family owned business? Do you want to stick to one piece of clothing, or do you want to expand your clothing options at some point? Do you want to make a commitment to sourcing all your clothing ethically no matter the cost or do you always want to go to a cost-effective way? These are the questions you want to ask yourself and these are the questions that you should consider while you are structuring your business. Dream as big as you can and do not limit yourself to what you just see now.

As a heads up, this will not be a major concern at the start your business. You will need to make sales first. If your business doesn't make sales than you don't have to pay taxes. You will have time to file your taxes. When you start making consistent sales then you will want to get that done. This chapter was just the legal stuff and what you need to get your foot in the door to the wholesalers. Your main focus will be in the chapters to come.

CHAPTER 2

BRANDING: IT IS NOT AS HARD AS YOU THINK

Branding is a big decision. Every business owner must decide what they want their brand to be. Your brand must be exciting, unique, and fit into your ideals. Your brand is important because it separates you from another company. Some people have very strict methodologies about what type of brand name is most successful for a clothing company. Some people have a strict list of do's and do not. However, I believe the proper branding for your company is whatever you truly feel you want to do. It is not as hard as you think. The branding should speak to the style that you want to make and sale. Many people have ideas for brands, but they are not sure about how to bring the idea to life. If you have purchased this book, then I'm sure you have already thought of an idea for a brand. This chapter will help you refine the branding idea that you already have or help you create a brand if you do not have one already. Initially, you want to start off with strong branding because the brand will be associated with your business for a very long time. The branding consists of the physical assets such as the colors and physical imaging of your branding, like your logo. Your brand is also abstract as it is the story behind your company. Two important components help determine what your branding will be. The first component is the brand concept or the idea for your business. The next component important to your brand is going to be your target market.

The idea behind your business is the brand concept. Simply put, the brand concept is about what your brand represents. To help form your brand concept, you will want to ask yourself a few important questions.

- When people see your brand, what ideas do you want them to associate with your brand? - Do you want them to think of youthfulness or maturity? Do you want them to think of free-spirited people or business-minded people? What other ideas do you want them to think about when they hear your brand's name or sees your brands imaging. There is no right or wrong answer for this. It is simply what you want your brand to be.
- What is your mission statement? - You may think a mission statement is a broad, detailed story, but it is simply what you want your company to do or be. What kind of goals do you want to reach with your company? Do you want to be top grossing baby line company in the world, or would you like to be the most successful luggage design company in the world? Do you want to help stop poverty with a portion of your sales? Whatever your goal is for your company that is what your mission statement should be.
- What is your brand story? - Your brand story is different from your mission statement; although they may share some

overlap. The brand Story talks about the origins of your company, whereas the mission talks about the goals of your company. You can incorporate your origin story or the initial idea that inspired you to start your company. People connect to a brand story because they can see themselves in the brand. Make sure that the brand story is written in a way that's relatable and truthful. It is a foundational aspect of your business.

- What colors do you want to represent your brand question? - Choosing the colors of your brand is very important. If your brand has a calm vibe, then you most likely will want a calm color to represent your brand. A fiery color like orange and red may not be ideal, but a cool color like blue or light green may be more ideal. However, there is no hard-and-fast rule for the colors that you choose. Your brand makes the color. Do not stress if your colors are like another business because there are only so many colors in the world, so a few businesses are bound to use the same kind. However, make sure that your colors represent your brand in a way that it is not used by another brand. That's where your brand story in your mission statement comes into play.

- What logo would you like to represent your brand? - Some people like to just use logos or initials to represent their brand. The type of font used in the logo is also part of the brand. There are lots of different companies that can help you develop your brand. A popular website to use is fiverr.com. There you can find freelance designers. You will be able to explain to them exactly what you want. You will be able to ask for revisions. Other people like to post logo design jobs on Upwork. A freelancing website where you can hire people for one job or for work. This is a more expensive option, only use this if your logo must be made by a digital artist.

Once you have your initial branding down, you will then want to think about your target market. They may influence your branding efforts as well. A great activity to do when trying to figure out who your target market is to create three brand identities of the people who will buy your product. This helps you to learn more about your customers and find a brand that will appeal to them. It is important to know multiple types of customers you are targeting because different target markets will be attracted to your business for different reasons. Knowing your target audience may help you prevent a no-no. For example, if you have a vegan company, you may not want to have a bloody cow as your logo. Thinking about your customer can help you come up with cool ideas and ways that you can connect to them. When trying to figure out who your target market is going to be, you want to do your research. You may realize that your idea may not work after you do research. However, these three brand identities will help you research further and find out more about your customer. It is important to note that when you begin, you will learn more about your customers. As the information comes in about who is buying your product, do not be afraid to adjust some of your branding efforts at the point.

When you think about the brand identities here are a few questions that you can ask.

- Where is your customer from? What country or continent are they from? What city in that country are they from?
- How old is your target demographic? Try to narrow this down as much as possible. Have one major segment and then another major segment for two major target demographics.
- Will your clothing solve a certain problem for them? Is your target demographic unable to find styles that work for them that your style will address? Are they unable to find clothes that match their style?
- Does your clothing represent a certain ideal for them? Is your clothing brand the exclusive like supreme or affordable and nice like H&M
- Where does your customer stay most of the time when they are on the internet? Are they browsing social media or are they on news websites?
- How do you get your promotion in front of them? Are you going to use advertisements on a search engine or social media websites?
- What are their hobbies? What do they love to do already? What hobbies are they spending money on to do?
- What do they like to read? What genres do they like to read? Do they prefer audiobooks, printed books, magazines, or blogs?

- What do they like to eat? Are they plant-based or love meat? Do they care about where the animals they eat come from?
- Are they healthy? Do they suffer from chronic illnesses?
- Are they married? Are they divorced? Are they in long-term relationships? Are they in homosexual or heterosexual relationships?
- Do they have children? How many? Are these children that they birthed? Are these children that they adopted? Do they have trouble conceiving?
- Are they homeowners? Or do they rent? What type of homes are they living in? Brownstones? Ranch homes
- What type of interior décor is their style? Modern? Farmhouse? Contemporary? Chic?
- Do they travel? Do they travel domestically or internationally?
- Are they educated? If so, how much education do they have? What's the highest education they have?
- What do they do for a living? Are they blue-collar or white-collar workers?
- Do they have pets? Do they have dogs or cats? Or fish?
- What type of cars do they drive? Do they love luxury, hybrids, practical?
- What movies do they watch? What're their favorite genres?
- What TV shows do they watch? Are they watching cable or a paid service like Netflix or Hulu?

Forming a detailed profile and multiple profiles will help you to make connections with your target market in ways that you would not have done had you not been as detailed. Be as detailed as possible and look for connections. It will help you market to them as well. The step should not be taken lightly. Take the time to sit and think through this. You can give yourself a few hours in a room with a pen and paper or with your computer to take notes. Do not have any distractions. Do not turn the TV on, and you can even turn your phone off. Having a very focused, niche target demographic can be the difference between success and failure. You can mark it to more than one target demographic. However, you must start with at least one target demographic first. Build on one target demographic, have success with that target demographic, and then move to the next target demographic. Next thing you know you will be selling to lots of people. Just remember that you must crawl before you walk.

Other factors to think about when you are branding include the niche of clothing that you want to sell. You also want to think about the quality of clothing that you want to sell. You will also want to think about the design of the clothing you want to sell. When you are choosing a niche, make sure that the target demographic is large enough for you to make sales. Having a specific niche will help you be more targeted in your marketing efforts and this Focus will help you to make more sales. Many people like to choose 18-65 as their target market, but that is just too broad. Try to break that market down and get as focused as possible. Remember the saying the riches are in the niches. When choosing your target demographic, also consider if you want to work with these types of customers. When you are selling you will have to engage customers at some point. So, make sure you feel comfortable with your target demographic to engage with them on a customer service level if necessary. Another important factor that can help you with branding is to consider the quality of clothing that you are selling. Make sure that your target demographic would like to buy the quality of clothing that you are selling. Lastly, consider the type of designs that you are selling. Some designs just do not look good on certain demographics. Be objective and open about what designs will best fit your target demographic. A great way to turn this principle on its head is to try and sell clothing that a certain target demographic is not used to having a great fit in. If you can help people feel a certain way, you are guaranteed to make money.

Start the company with a solid brand is more important than letting your brand stop you from getting started. These three brand identities are a great place to start, and it will help you research further and find out more about your customer. If you have the money for it, you can also hire a brand consultant to do the heavy lifting for you. If you have local business accelerators in your city or an SBA office or any nonprofit that helps economic development in the city, they may have workshops for developing your brand. So be sure to take advantage of these free opportunities to get feedback about your business. Once you have a solid brand concept, it is important to move to the next step which is figuring out what type of business model is best for your clothing company.

CHAPTER 3

THE BEST BUSINESS MODEL FOR YOUR CLOTHING BUSINESS

Now that you have your business registered and your branding taken care of, you now must figure out the logistics behind your business. In other words, you need to figure out how to bring your clothing business to life. What business model is going to best to help your ideas come to life? How you go about manufacturing your clothing line is dependent upon a few factors including your skill level, how much money you have, and what your values are. In this chapter, we will discuss different options to bring your clothing designs to the real world so you can sell them. We will discuss cut and sew manufacturers, print-on-demand manufacturers, blank manufacturers, and blank wholesalers. By the time you finish with this chapter, you will have a better idea of which logistics method and business model to use to start your business. Many options will require upfront costs, so do not skimp on these costs or begrudge them. Rather, think of the expenses you have as an investment for your businesses. The old business adage is true, "You must spend money to make money." However, most of the options benefit from the economies of scale. So the more you order, the cheaper the overall costs will be, so keep that in mind.

The first way to start your clothing business is with a cut and sew manufacturer. This is ideal if you want to design unique one-of-a-kind pieces that are exclusive that you cannot find anywhere else. This will be great if you want to make avant-garde pieces or if you want to make timeless handcrafted pieces. The cut and sew manufacturing option requires a lot of upfront work and a lot of money. When you choose this option, you oversee creating the designs, turning the designs into patterns, finding the fabric that you want to use for your designs, and creating samples of your designs. After you have the samples, you then must research and find a manufacturer to create your designs, then you will order a full production run. This can take months to get a final design before the design is even manufactured in bulk. If you do not have the basic skills of sewing or fashion designing, you can assemble a team to help you bring your designs to life. There are a lot of different manufacturers you can use for this type of design whether they be overseas or local

If this is your first attempt using a cut and sew manufacturer, I STRONGLY recommend using a local manufacture. Local manufactures are better to you in this case because you can meet with them in person and talk about what you want in fine detail. You can even be as hands on with them with what you want. The easiest way to find a cut and sew manufacturer is to Google 'cut and sew manufacturer' and your city name. If you have limited funds, you can also Google, 'cut and sew manufacturers low minimum.' Be sure to look at all the information that is not on the first page. You can find gems hidden in the less popular pages.

If you cannot make clothes yourself but can make designs, you will need to hire a sample maker to bring your idea to life. The sample maker will be able to sketch your idea and make your design. Your design is important because every part of the clothes must be drawn and broken down for the manufacturer to process the design in order to produce it. When the design is on paper, the individual pattern can be created along with the measurements and shapes of the design. All this needs to be included so the manufacturer can mass produce your designs. If you are unable to cut and sew yourself, then you must use a sample maker, you will have to pay for the sample. However, the sample will be worth it because you can see your work come to life. If you need to find a sample maker, try and Google local pattern makers in your city. You can also find freelance pattern makers from sites like Fiverr.com or upwork.com. Another great place to find a sample maker would be to check out fashion forums for their recommendation. Some cut and sew manufacturers have pattern makers on staff so when you are researching the cut and sew manufacturer that you want to use see if they have any people on site. Another thing to keep in mind is that a pattern maker does not have to have professional experience as this industry is not regulated. So, you have to do your own research when deciding on who you want to work with on your patterns. An excellent patternmaker can help you find the perfect fit for your customers.

A few questions to keep in mind when vetting pattern makers would be as follows. You must determine if you want them to sign a non-disclosure and non-compete agreement. You want to look at their samples and see what type of clients they worked at with. Again, you want to budget for the most experienced pattern maker that you can afford. How did you feel connecting with them?

Do they have any recommendations? These few questions can help you figure out if you want a relationship with the pattern maker or not.

The second business model is not as involved as the cut and sew process. If your clothing company only requires a small logo or graphic design work that requires embroidery or printing, only, here are the few routes you can take to fit your needs. The start-up costs are a lot cheaper, as well. They are easier to learn. A lot of people are using these methods, so they are also more competitive. However, if you have a targeted niche, you can still make money.

The first service is called print on demand, and it works like this. First, you upload a graphic design to a print on demand site and set the design up on different products like shirts, sweatshirts, mugs posters, or whatever products the print on demand site offers. Then you position the design on the products just how you want. And then choose to put the products on sale. Second, you can post the design to your company's website. Third, when somebody orders your print on demand piece, the print-on-demand company will receive the customers' information, the size they way, their address, and company, and will produce the product and ship the order for you. You will not have to do anything, except upload your design and position it on the products. The print on demand company fulfills the order, and this method is completely passive. Some print-on- demand companies offer customized features, like customized tags so you can better brand your clothes.

The pros of this method are that you do not have to order a lot number of items upfront and you can let them handle fulfilling all the orders. The cons to print on demand are the royalties you receive and the restriction on your design placements and blank items you can use. The print on demand company takes a portion of your sale. Another advantage with this method is that you do not have to have your own site, you can just use their site to sell your items. Another con is that you are limited to the types of merchandise that they have on their sites. Overall, this is a much lower risk because you do not have to order large quantities of clothing and worry about putting them in a warehouse! There are no minimum orders and the company only prints what the customer wants so you do not have the risk of having extra, unwanted inventory. Popular print on demands sites are services like Printful, Zazzle, Printify, or Print Aura to name a few. More print-on-demand services are being started every day with each company having differing offerings. You can take your designs and put them on various blank items like shirts, sweatshirt, and other options like mugs. Really, the options are endless. So, you just must research and see which company offers the print-on-demand selection that you prefer.

The next option to bring your clothes to life is to use blank manufacturers. With blank manufacturers, they have more variety than a print-on-demand company. They offer to put your custom designs on a wider variety of blanks with more customized options for branding. The difference between this service and print on demand is that you must order wholesale and fulfill the orders yourself. This means that if you must order a larger minimum order, then find a place to house the items. Many big brands like thrasher do this kind of manufacturing. We will talk more about that in future chapters. The pro to this type of manufacturing is that there is a wider variety of design options to make your brand more unique and stand out more. You also can get items at a lower cost because you are ordering wholesale. However, you must have a place to keep your inventory and then send the orders out yourself.

The last type of manufacturing option is called blank wholesaler. This takes the blank manufacturer to another level. This is also great to use is you have access to a large amount of capital and have lots of orders to fulfill. This allows you to get a greater return on your investment. For this type of manufacturing, you buy blank materials from companies that specialize in blanks. There are blank companies that can specialize in shirts, pants, or whatever type of clothing you are interested in designing. Once you purchase from them, you can ship the blanks to other tailors or manufactures and they will add materials you want to add to the blank clothing such as ribbons, embroidery, patches, and graphic prints onto them. However, you will have to supply the other accessories to the supplier. After they add the extra materials to your clothing, then they will send you the completed products. Or you can do it yourself if you please.

At that point, you can house the products in a warehouse and then you must fulfill every order yourself if you are selling the products from your individual website. However, if you were to use a third-party website like Amazon to sell your products, you can ship the materials to an Amazon warehouse, and they will fulfill the orders for you. This means that they will house your product and anytime anyone orders your product from Amazon, Amazon will ship it for you. However, there are costs to have your orders fulfilled by Amazon but the program for that is called fulfilled by Amazon or FBA. If you are going to house the warehouse items yourself, you have to find a warehouse (can be your garage or somewhere else) that you can hold it if you can't hold it at your house or business. Then you will have to hire someone to send out the orders every time someone orders from you. You can purchase fulfillment services and warehouse services, so you do not have to fulfill orders yourself. However, you must make sure that you have a lot of customers for this type of service to work so your profits will not be consumed by the warehouse and fulfillment costs.

A multi-tiered approach to creating manufacturing and fulfilling your orders are recommended. If you do not have a lot of money upfront you can always start with print-on-demand and then work your way up to other services depending on your orders. You can also consider selling direct sales clothing. These type of clothing companies are like Mary Kay. You find a company that you want to sell their clothing. Then you can host different parties to sell the clothing to your friends. This business model is all about relationship marketing. The beauty of this business model is usually low cost to start and you can make a profit easily. The other great thing about this model is you can find all types of clothing options to choose from. If you want to do women's clothing, baby clothing, men's clothing lingerie, shapewear, anything you want, there is most likely a direct clothing company that sells it. You just have to find one and make sure that it matches to your target audience. The other beautiful thing about this model is that you can use the profits from this business to reinvest into your business. Then when your clothing line is up and going you can begin selling your clothes to the customers that are already buying your direct sales clothing. It is a definite win-win.

Whatever option you choose, you must make sure that you are researching the different options and you have a capital to make your money back. Also, do not be afraid to build on the different models. Your business can consist of using different models to learn the capital that will allow you to become a cut and sew manufacturer. Do not view these models as you can only do one. You can do more than one and take advantage of all the business models that are available today. Once you figure out the best way to create your designs and fulfill them, that's when your real fun begins. Because then, you can repeat the process over and over again with as many designs as you like and feel the joy of lots of different people wearing your clothes.

CHAPTER 4

Laying The Ground Work: Clothing And Fabric Fundamentals

When you are trying to decide what type of clothing to sell, it is always good to think about what type of clothes you like and what feels good to you. You can use this as a baseline but remember your customers may not have the same tastes as you. It is important to understand what the different cloth and fabric feel like. Then you will be able to design clothing that your target demographic will love. When you are deciding who to sell your clothes too, you want to be mindful of their body shape and what fabrics work best for their body types. People will not want to buy clothing from you if they do not look good in it, so be mindful of the type of clothes that look good on your target demographics body type. This chapter covers the basics of fabric design so when you are sourcing the fabric in your clothes you can have a deeper understanding of what type of fabric you are selecting. The chapter is essentially a quick glossary of manufacturing terms that you can access any times you have questions about a term that you aren't familiar with. Be sure to bookmark it because you may need it as we continue further in the book.

Manufacturing Terms

Cut and sew- This is the manufacturing method that the makers of designer clothes use. This manufacturing method requires you to pick out the measurements of everything. You also must consider the measurements of materials that are added to the basic design like ribbons, straps or pockets. This is the most advanced style of clothing design and requires some studying.

Embroidery- This art form is the process of creating patterns or drawings that are then sown onto your clothes.

Blanks- These are clothes that have flat colors such as flat black, white, green, red or whatever color you want. You can order these clothes in bulk and then add your own design, branding, style, screen print, or embroidery. The blanks can come in multiple clothing styles like shirts, bags, stickers, purses, etc.

Prints- A print is when you create a design and then add the print design on the front of the shirt. Screen-printing is one of the most known version of printing that is applied to t-shirts. Screen print services normally only have room for printing on the front of your shirt. There may be extra costs with trying to print on the back.

Fabrics- There are many fabrics you can use for your clothing designs. You will have much more freedom to use the fabric that you want once you get into cut and sew manufacturing.

Here's a brief lesson into fabric fundamentals.

Fabrics come in two styles.

The first style is called woven. Woven styles are not stretchy. They are not good for good for fitted styles. The second style of fabric is called knit. A knit style consists of fabric that is stretchy.

There are different types of fabrics that are made from natural materials, or materials from nature, synthetic materials, or materials made by humans, or semi-synthetic materials, or materials made with a combination of natural and synthetic materials.

Natural Fabrics

- Cotton: Cotton is grown from the cotton plant. It is considered fluffy, soft and a staple fiber of many clothing styles. It is breathable.
- Linen: Linen is made from the fibers of the flax plant. Linen is difficult to manufacture, but once manufactured, the fiber is extremely strong, very absorbent and tends to dry more quickly than cotton. Linen garments are noted for being very cool and fresh in humid and hot weather.
- Silk: Silk fabric is well-known across the globe as being a textile of high luxury. It is made from silkworms.
- Cashmere: Cashmere is a fiber that is collected from cashmere goats and other types of goats. Most people call it a wool but is it softer and finer than sheep's wool.
- Hemp: Hemp has three times the tensile strength as cotton, which means it is more durable than cotton. It is absorbent and lightweight.

Synthetic Fabrics

Nylon: Nylon is a general term for polymers that are made synthetically, based on semi-aromatic or aliphatic polyamides. A silky, thermoplastic silky material, nylon can be melted and then processed into shapers, films or fibers.

Acrylic: Acrylics are used for tracksuits, linings in gloves and boots and sweaters because they are warm and strong. Acrylic is also often used in carpet and as furnishing fabrics. It is made like a filament and then cut into short and staple lengths. These lengths are like wool hairs and then they spin it into yarn.

Polyester: Polyester is made in a variety of things from clothes to home furnishings to even industrial fibers, yarns, and ropes. Polyester can be used in hats, bed sheets, blankets, computer mouse mats, jackets and hats, upholstered furniture, car tire reinforcements, conveyor belts, coated fabrics, and safety belts.

Spandex: Spandex is known for being stretchy and it is a synthetic fiber.

Semi-Synthetic Fibers

Rayon: Rayon is sometimes called artificial silk. and it is used as a substitution for silk. It also was the first semi-synthetic fiber created.

Lyocell: This fiber is similar to other fibers like linen, ramie, cotton and viscose rayon. The common characteristics that these cellulosic fibers share is that they are wrinkle-resistant, strong no matter if they are wet or dry, absorbent and soft.

Fashion Terms

Haute Couture: This is French for fine tailoring. It is very expensive. Prices can range from $2,000 to $40,000. It is made with individuals in mind.

Mass Market: Clothing that is designed for the masses. The sizes are more general, and the materials cost less money. They are also cheaply produced.

Designer Label: These clothes are a combination between haute couture and mass market. The clothing is more expensive and created in smaller batches to have a level of exclusivity.

Fashion: The prevailing style of clothing that is popular.

Fad: A style that experiences a sudden burst in popularity.

Style: A distinct form that develops irrespective of the current fashion trends.

Classic: A fashion that is in style over time.

Design: A certain style of fashion. This can refer to popular cuts of certain clothing.

Trend: The time that a style is popular in a marketplace.

Important Facts To Know

A fashion year has two main seasons. The first season is a spring and summer season. The next season is an autumn and winter season. The spring and summer season are all about light fabrics and the autumn and winter seasons utilize heavier fabrics.

Designers work a year in advance. In the spring and summer, they are working on next spring and summers collections. Their difficult task is to try and predict what items will work well.

There are lots of fashionable places, but the most important fashion centers consist of five cities. Milan, Italy, is known for luxurious and casual elegance. Paris, France, is known for its chic and stylish styles. London, England, is known for its young market and non-traditional fashion choices. New York City, New York, is known for clean-cut casual clothing. Tokyo, Japan, is known for its loose and unstructured clothing. The fabrics are usual somber and rich in texture.

Popular Italian Designers

  Fendi

  Max Mara

  Dolce E Gabbana

  Giorgio Armani

  Salvatore

Popular French Designers

  Chanel

  Givenchy

  Valentino

  Christian Dior

  Yves Saint-Laurent

Popular English Designers

  Vivienne Westwood

Ghost

Pam Hogg

Betty Jackson

Nick Coleman

Popular American Designers

Calvin Klein

Donna Karan

Ralph Lauren

Tom Ford

Bill Blass

Popular Japanese Designers

Jin Abe

Issey Miyake

Junko Kishino

Hiroko Kishino

Hanae Mori

These are the basics that can help you get started with designing your clothes. Learning as much as you can about clothing and fabric terminology will only help you in the long run. If you come off as if you do not know what you are talking about, manufacturers may try to take advantage of that. The more informed you appear; people will know that they cannot take advantage of you. So, as you are learning, try to get a second opinion whenever is necessary so you come off as informed. The most important thing is to not view learning as a task.

This is your business and your dream. Have fun with it and learn something new every day.

CHAPTER 5

GRAPHIC DESIGN AND CLOTHING DESIGN: WHAT YOU NEED TO KNOW

Art comes in as many forms. That's the beauty of art and the beauty of working with clothing. Clothing is wearable art that people wear to show the world a little about themselves. The colors, designs, and types of clothing that people wear in different combinations express how they feel. There is no right or wrong way to express yourself with clothing. If you are lucky, people will fall in love with what you have to say through your designs and happily wear it. For some people, their goal is to have their clothing brand be worn by the masses and for others they want their clothing brand to be worn by a selective few. Whatever your goal is for your clothing brand, you will utilize the arts of graphic design and fashion designing to help express bring your designs into fruition.

The first tool that you want to familiarize yourself with when you are designing your clothing is graphic design. Graphic design is important because it allows us to use our creative expression on a platform that connects virtually everyone in the entire world. Graphic design is a skill that is important when doing logos, advertisement, and t-shirt designs. Adobe Illustrator is an industry-standard that many people like to use when graphic designing. Adobe Photoshop and

Adobe InDesign are also two other popular software tools that graphic designers like to use which are also industry standards. To learn more about using these products, you can watch tutorials on YouTube or take courses using Skillshare. Other graphic designing platforms that are easy to work with for beginners include LunaPic, Canva, and Gimp, all web-based platforms and free. These websites also come with individual tutorials that can help you acclimate to their platform. When you work with graphic design, then you will be able to work more with blanks. This skill will allow you to make more money in the long-term. Just like any skill once you understand the basics the more you practice the better you become. Even if you are not familiar with graphic design if you understand a few basics you will be able to practice and become better.

Once you understand the basics of graphic design then you will be able to choose which principle you want to use in your designs. You can use all the principles in one design, or you can select a few principles to bring out the point that you are trying to make. The fun part of graphic design is understanding the principles. Often people think that great designers are just talented, and they come up with everything from scratch. While yes, great graphic designers are talented, but they have a basic understanding of graphic design principles. They are then able to use those principles to get the great designs that they want. You too can be a great designer. However, you should learn the basics. Remember, if you have to pay someone for these, you may have to pay a pretty penny, especially if they are talented. Make an investment in yourself and in your business by learning the skills. That way you will be able to do designs yourself in the future. Once you understand them, then you can play around to get the design that you want. You can truly let your imagination run wild. You will also find that people can love designs that you are not fond of, but remember, the customer is always right. Make the designs that are selling not the ones that are your personal favorites.

The first principle of graphic design is color. When you are designing a graphic, it is important to note how the colors will affect what you are trying to say. Do the colors match? Are you trying to represent a certain mood? The colors you use will help draw attention to the design based on what you are trying to say. If you want a classic design, you should avoid bold colors and stick to neutral colors. If you are trying to be bold in your design, you want to use bright and neon colors. If you want people to be more relaxed when they see your graphics, you use calming colors. If you want to have them energized after they see your design, you will use colors that energize. If you understand the importance of color, then you have mastered the first principle of graphic design.

The next principle of graphic design is called repetition. Repetition is an important design concept because when used effectively it can bring organization to a design. You can also use repetition to help your design be memorable. I'm sure you can think of popular brands that use repetition of their logo on their products. Repetition is also an effective tool to use in branding.

Contrast is the next design principle. It is a useful tool when trying to draw attention to something in your design. Opposites work well is the basis of this design principle. For example, long lines and short lines can form interesting design as well as using the contrast of black-and-white. Utilizing opposites in your design can make for interesting concepts.

The fourth design principle is called alignment. This graphic design principle is all about aligning fonts and colors together to make a statement. Using alignment also helps your design to come out neat and organized, not sloppy and disheveled. Creative uses of alignment against more free-flowing background can draw attention to the main element in the design. Oftentimes, the graphic tools that you design have graph lines that you can use to help organize your graphic to make sure the design is aligned and neat. Being aligned also adds a level of professionalism to your graphic designs.

Proximity is another design principle that when used well it makes your design look professional, and it is the fifth design principle. The idea behind proximity is that all similar information is grouped together in the design. The information that is grouped can be grouped based on color, content, fonts, or even shape. When you find ways to group similar information, it helps a powerful statement be made, and it helps people not to miss information that you may be trying to construe.

The sixth design principle is called hierarchy. This helps you to place the most important information in a more prominent position than lesser important information. To bring the most important information to the forefront you can use bigger fonts or higher placement on the graphic design. When you want to use this design principle, you first want to think about what information is the most important that you want to convey. Then use hierarchy to make that information stand out.

Balance is the seventh design principle. This does not mean that everything is equal. It means that you are professionally spacing out all the information in the design so that it looks professional. Balance allows the viewer not to be overwhelmed with information. For example, if you are using a lot of strong and bold colors. Balancing out your fonts can help emphasize the statement that you are trying to make. It helps bring stability to the design and balances all the elements, so it won't feel overwhelming. Balancing out the design makes it more pleasurable to the eye.

The last design element is called spacing. This design element allows the design to breathe. Being strategic where you include space in your design can cause a pop of contrast or it can bring more attention to a particular element. You remember the saying, 'Less is more.'? Spacing is like this saying. Use space wisely in your design so it does not appear jumbled and lose the viewer.

Once you understand these basic principles, you are able to create the designs that you want. One of the easiest ways to get better at graphic design is to look at good designs when you are looking at different fashions and graphics. Magazines are great examples of good design. When you see a design that you like, what are you drawn to? When you see something that you are drawn to, try to figure out what attracts you to that design? Think about what principles they are using on that design. Then you can try to utilize it in your own design.

Looking at good design and identifying what elements the design is using helps you create your own design theory and helps you to make your own designs more unique.

Cut and sew designing is another tool you want to learn if you want to truly make your clothing company stand out. If you have zero experience in this field, but you want to learn how to cut and sew in order to make great clothes for people, then you can learn. Great resources to use would be YouTube and Skillshare. You do not have to be a professional tailor, but you will have to have a certain level of skill to be able to properly communicate with people who can. If you understand the basics of cut and sew design, you will be able to better relay your ideas.

If you have no idea but you still want to design clothes, then you might want to hire a designer. The designer will make the design for your clothes from your inspiration. If you do not want to hire a designer, then you then want to work with your manufacture closely to get the perfect sample made. Once you get a sample of what you want, then they will be able to reproduce that piece of clothing. Therefore, the sample is the most important part of the manufacturing process. If the sample is wrong and the factory reproduces it, your entire order will be according to that sample and therefore wrong.

If you are interested in learning more about cut and sew and design here are a few places where you can begin. You will first want to learn how to design your Creations. This means knowing how to put the initial idea on paper. This is one of the very first tips to learn. Then you can learn others things that can be helpful, like:

- How to make patterns from your designs
- How to put your pattern markings on the fabric
- How to thread a needle or a sewing machine
- How to sew darts buttons and the perfect seams
- How to sew flat-felled seams and French scenes,
- How to sew corners and other directional sewing
- How to create a face pattern
- How to hem
- How to sew a set in a sleeve
- How to gather versus ease
- How to sew flack and shank buttons
- How to do under stitching
- How to tailor and how to grade a scene

If you learn these basics you will be well on your way to cut and sew and design. You can learn one skill at a time. You do not have to feel overwhelmed. If cut and sew designing is something you are interested in, think of it as a marathon, not a sprint. The more you can cut and design on your own, the more you will be able to save costs in the long run. However, some people have no interest in learning how to cut and sew design for their clothing company and that is okay. In that case, they want to hire a designer. Similar to hiring a pattern maker, there are a few questions you want to consider when you are hiring a designer.

One of the first things you want to consider when hiring a designer is your budget. Most of the time, the more budget you have, the better designer you will be able to use. However, there are ways to find a cheaper designer, but know that the quality of your clothing may suffer. If you need haute couture you want to spend more money on the designer, but if you are just looking for someone to design a t-shirt you may be able to skip on the designer. If you are looking for more affordable designers, you can look for freelancers on Fiverr or upwork.com or freelancer.com. To cut cost, you may also see if you can find a student fashion designer that will be willing to work for you.

Note that a proficient designer can cost anywhere from $35 to $40 per hour. The more pieces you have in the collection, the more experience you would you are your designer to have. Also, the more experience and education the designer has, the more expensive the designer will be. Once you find a designer that you want to use, you will need to look at their portfolio.

- What do you think about their other work?
- Do they know about fabrics or sourcing fabrics or will you have to do that?
- Do they know about the latest trends?
- What is there a fashion philosophy?
- Do you agree with it?
- Is your designer well-connected in the industry to the point where they know what's going on?
- Does the designer know how to use design software?
- What experiences do they have in fashion designing?

- What type of education do they have? Sometimes more experience is more important than the education. You just must see what about the designer speaks to you in order to make that determination.

Once you have selected a designer, you can then get a second opinion. See if they can make a sample for you and then find someone else that you trust to look at the quality. If you do not want him to make a sample for you, see if they can do a sketch. That's a great way to look at their design skills as well.

After you have decided to hire a designer now you need to hold your end of the bargain. Make sure that you are signing agreements to protect the confidentiality of your work. Also, pay your designer on time and well. Let the designer has some type of freedom so they can do their job well. Also, be open to providing ongoing support and training with them. The most important tip no matter if it is with the designer or a pattern maker or a manufacturer is to have excellent communication. Make sure that they can respond promptly and make sure that you are responding promptly as well. Be in touch with every part of the design process so you can catch mistakes as they come along.

Before you even contact the designer, you should have all the research done about your collection. This includes the types of fabric that you want to use and the customer you want to buy your products. You should be mindful of color trends, fabric trends, sourced fabrics, trend color grouping, mood boards, and trend reports. To have a 10-

style collection designed can cost anywhere from $300 to $1,200 USD. After the collection is complete, the next step you want to do is get the designer to design sketches for you.

For more pieces and even to share their ideas with you, a fashion designer can charge anywhere from $500 to $1,000 for a 10-piece collection. This will consist of the black and white sketches. After this is approved, the designer will then create the cad flats. This is what the pattern makers and manufacturers need in order to create your products. There needs to be a front and back of the garment for the designer software. This step can cost anywhere from $300 - $800.

Now it is time for the most expensive part of the process which is to get the industry patterns. This is what you need to make sure the patterns are up to date with American sizes. The more separate pieces, collars, seams, design layers, collars, pockets, and sleeves, you have in a garment, the more it costs for the pattern. If the design is going to be lined, that's going to cost more, too. If you need to have a fitting of people to try your clothes on, which I recommend, add that on. It is best to have your pattern created on paper first and keep that in a safe place. That way you can always have it transferred to a digital pattern for different sizes if needed later. The designer can charge anywhere from $85 -$800 per pattern. If you have 10 pieces in your collection, that can quickly add up.

After this is created, you then you will have to go to the pattern maker. If you do not want to do this yourself, you can hire the designer to go back and forth with the pattern maker. Of course, it will be an extra charge for you. They may even have a pattern maker that they are already used to working with. After they go to the pattern maker, you must account for that time as well. Like any good professional, if they are good, they are going to be busy. So, you can expect that one pattern can take anywhere from 4 days to a week to get made.

You will want to make sure that the pattern is correct. Again, you can hire the designer to go back and forth with the pattern maker to bring your pattern to life. The cost for any extras on the design, like ribbons or embroidery, are not going to be added in the cost, so you must pay for that.

You will next want to have a tech pack made. This can raise the price from $800 to $6,000 on the upper end. Now after everything comes out well, then you can use the pattern overseas with a manufacturer. This is how overseas manufacturers know what to make from your clothing. This can take anywhere from $700 to $6000 USD. On the lower end, getting your entire fashion line designed by a fashion designer will take about $10,000. You also want to account for DMT, which is a designer's management time. This is the time that accounts for the back and forth with the pattern maker or any errands that they run. Most designers charge 40% of their overall price for DMT. Do not skimp on the pricing, especially if you want a valuable designer.

Graphic designing and cut-and-sew designing are two important tools that you can use to help bring your designs to life. Graphic designing and cut-and-sew designing are advanced designing skills. The more you know, the better your business will be. Hence, you should consider investing in a few classes to learn more. You can investigate classes at your community college or looking for free courses online. To save costs, you can even consider becoming an apprentice at a local sewing shop or you can find someone who can sew and see if they are willing to teach you. If this is a business that you are committed to, you should make an investment to learn as much as you can. Your business will only thrive as a result. Thankfully, we live in a time where there are many different options you can use to make your designs a reality. It is just up to you to make the decision about which one you want to use.

CHAPTER 6

CREATE YOUR COMPANY'S WEBSITE THE EASY WAY

The next important aspect of your clothing business that you want to consider is your website. Your website is an important draw in bringing people to you. There are a few different ways to help bring your website to life. You also want to make sure that your website ties into your branding. If you have certain colors in your logo, you want your website to reflect those colors as well. You want to make sure that you are using a similar font on your website that's in your logo. That way you have a consistent branding message no matter where they see an asset advertising your business. The types of options you use for your website or depending upon your budget and your technical skill. It also depends on how much time you have and what type of tools you want to take advantage of. This chapter is all about ways to design your website. We will discuss a few different ways to create your website, including Shopify, Big Cartel, WordPress, and hiring a graphic designer to build your website.

One of the most popular ways to create your business's website is to use Shopify. Shopify is highly recommended because many people already use it, and they have many great back office tools. Shopify also easily connects to many print-on- demand services easily. Shopify has a free two-week trial that you can use, but in order to sell on your website, you will need to pay at least the minimum pricing to have access to the selling features. Using Shopify is a very popular option. Many successful companies use Shopify. There is a lot of support from the Shopify website itself, along with Shopify communities, blogs, and tutorials about how to use Shopify. Therefore, if you go with this option, you will not fail for a lack of information.

Currently, Shopify has three different tiers. The first year is the basic tee, and it cost $29 a month. The next tier is $79 a month, and the highest tier is $229 US dollars a month. Every Shopify tier allows you to create discount codes and sell unlimited products on your website. It also gives you a way to email people if they abandon their cart, and it protects your website from hackers with an SSL certificate. This certificate is needed to protect the credit card information of people that by your products. The higher Shopify tier you purchase, the more bells and whistles you have access to.

Shopify has a payment system built in that they charge you to use. It is built in so you will want to adjust your pricing to account for their processing chargers. If you are using the most basic tier of Shopify, anytime you make a sell, you pay 2.9% plus 30 cents if the customer is using an online credit card. If you have the first tier, and the customer is paying in person, then you only pay they only pay 2.7% of the price. If the customer is using any other payment method, there is a 2% charge. If you are using the second Shopify tier, anytime you make a sell online, you pay 2.6% plus 30 cents if they are using an online credit card. If you are using the second Shopify tier, you only pay 2.5% plus 30 cents if the customer is using a credit card in person, but if they are using any other payment method, then there is a 1% charge. If you are using the third Shopify tier anytime you make a sell online, you pay 2.4% plus 30 cents if they are using an online credit card. If they are using an in-person credit card they only pay 2.74%, and if they are using any other payment method is a 0.5% charge. With all the tiers, you can print shipping labels which makes your order fulfillment easier. Shopify is relatively easy to use, and it has a lot of bells and whistles in the backdrop. If you ever want to customize your Shopify website, you can either buy a theme or use the free themes that they have to customize your website.

If you want to buy a domain name to represent your business, you can use your Shopify store with that domain name. Shopify also has 24/7 our support for any questions you may have which is a major perk. If you want to sell just on your social media platforms, without having a Shopify website, you could consider Shopify Lite. This does not give you the option to create your own Shopify store, but it is a lot cheaper than the basic plan and it starts off at $9 a month. Depending on what country you are in determines how you will be paid. You can connect your PayPal or your bank account to Shopify. And for US customers, every two days Shopify will put your profits into your bank account or PayPal account. You also need to be aware that the fees will be taken out of your payments before it is deposited into your account.

Anytime you are setting up an online presence to take payments, you must be mindful of the fees that you may be charged. Some websites e-commerce websites charge a fee just to use their payment processing. Payment processing is important because it is a secured way to accept payments, and you do not have to worry about setting a secure way to process money on your own which can be a strenuous process. So, you have to be aware of the fees that your e-commerce processing may charge. For example, if they are using a payment processor like PayPal or Stripe, they will take a fee of the cost and the website will take the processing fee, too. These fees are minimal, but they can still add up. You should also make sure that the payment processor or the e-commerce site you are using does not have any minimum processing requirements. Some require that you make a certain amount of sales every month, or they will charge you a fee. When examining the site, that you want to use to set up your business, be mindful of that. In order to make the most money, you want to make sure that you have the most options for your customer to make a payment with, too. Not everyone has PayPal, not everyone has Stripe, and not everyone has a Visa. If you have the majority of payment options, then you will be okay. You also want to think about if you going to accept cashier's checks or personal checks. Most payment processors are also safeguarding you against fraud, so you do not have to worry about accepting payments from fraudulent credit cards. If you wanted to find any extra designers for hire in setting up your Shopify store, there is a marketplace for you to get assistance.

It is also rather easy to connect print-on-demand websites to Shopify. After you create your Shopify store, there is a place for you to select apps to connect to your Shopify in the back office. A popular print-on-demand app to use is called Printful. To connect it, you would need to login to Shopify. Then select the Apps option. When you select the apps, you will select the Printful app and connect your store to Printful. You will be required to submit your billing information, which you should do at that time. Next, you want to make sure that the products you are selling on Printful are already listed in your Shopify store. If they are already listed that's perfect. Anytime you are adding a product, remember that a variant is the same product, but just a different version of the product. For example, shirt sizes are variants of a certain shirt. Or the color of the shirt is a different variant. So, when you create your products make sure that you have all the necessary variants listed. Once your products are created, then you will go to your Printful app in your Printful account. In the back surface of Printful, you go to the store and then click on products. At this point, your Shopify products should show up in the Printful interface. You can then select the products from your Shopify store that you want to be fulfilled by Printful. You will be asked about the information and the picture of the product. Once that information is added, you are finished. Once set up, any item that is on your Shopify is now fulfilled by Printful. Other print-on-demand apps that you can use with Shopify are Printify, Teelaunch, Gooten, Pillow Profits, Print Aura, and Viralstyle. The good thing about Shopify is that new apps are being added daily that allows you to fulfill print-on-demand products. Most of these apps have a similar process to Printful that you add the app to your Shopify store. Shopify is a robust first choice option that many people choose to use, and with good reason.

Another option that you can use for your print-on-demand store is Big Cartel. Printful also connects to Big Cartel in the back end. Big Cartel is an e-commerce website that was made with artists and creatives in mind. Their price is not quite as expensive as Shopify. Their pricing tiers start off a little bit cheaper than Shopify, Big Cartel does have a limit on how many products you can upload to the site. Where is Shopify having unlimited products no matter which tier you purchase, Big Cartel's first tier is free, but it only consists of 5 products. When you start selling more than five products, then you must pay. The next level on Big Cartel of 25 products costs $9.99 a month; to sell a hundred products, it costs $19.99 a month; to sell 300 products, it costs $29.99 Big Cartel does not take a portion of your payments for processing, but they have a limited number of payment options they accept. They only accept Stripe and PayPal as payments. So you will only be responsible for the fees that PayPal and Stripe require. It I s2.75% for Stripe and 2.9% + $0.30 for PayPal. Shopify also has many integrations that you can use compared to Big Cartel. Big Cartel also has standard themes, but you can change the themes for free as well

The next way to create your website is to use WordPress. WordPress is a free software you can use to create your website. There are lots of free integrations you can use to customize your website, such as themes. You can choose a free theme or buy premium things to give your store the look you want. Once you have your WordPress account created, you will then need to use a plug-in that allows your WordPress site to take payments. A popular plug-in that's free and that many people use is called WooCommerce. While WooCommerce is free to customize the website, you have to pay for more plug-ins. If you want to accept lots of payments other than the Stripe and PayPal that comes with WooCommerce, you can add other plugins like authorize.net for $79 at the time of this writing. However, keep in mind that PayPal accepts all types of credit cards. You can also accept, Square and Amazon payments too when using WooCommerce. However, the tricky part with creating a WordPress site is to always make sure it is up to date to prevent hacks. Also, unlike an e-commerce site like Big Cartel or Shopify, you will need purchase an SSL certificate in order to accept payments. An SSL certificate secures your sit so it can accept payments. You can also add extra plugins for security on your website. Unlike Big Cartel and Shopify, you will have to be diligent in making sure the security on your site is up to date if you go the WordPress Option. However, it is a much cheaper option because you are not paying a monthly fee. You also want to have a backup of your site and use strong passwords so security can be top notch. Some people do not want to deal with the security issues that could potentially happen, so they avoid using WordPress. But just like Big Cartel and Shopify, if you go the WordPress option, you can have your own domain name. Making sure that your domain and hosting is reputable is another major way to protect security. However, if you do not mind the challenge, WordPress has lots of forums where you can learn information. Their support isn't as friendly for people who are not tech-savvy. You have to find solutions on your own, so it is a very DIY approach.

A quick note about domain names. A domain name is just the name of your website. You can purchase one from a domain name seller or hosting seller. A domain name is what allows your domain name to come on the internet. Then to turn it on the show it will show up when people visit your domain name is called hosting. Sites like Big Cartel or Shopify already pay for hosting so you just point the sites to your domain name. This means that when your domain name is typed in it will go straight to your Shopify or Big Cartel store instead of the longer name that you get when you sign up for free. Some people like to have a matching domain name with their brand without the Shopify or Big Cartel details in their domain name. For others, they want to save money, so they keep the name that Shopify or Big Cartel gives them when they open their store. It is totally up to you which option you think is best. However, if you do build a site from scratch, you must power that website to turn it on by buying a hosting package. There are certain different hosting packages that help your company handle the volume that you may receive. Popular hosting websites to visit are Bluehost, Namecheap, or even Go Daddy. All three approaches also have a way for you to add fulfillment apps to make sure that when people play their orders you can track and make sure that they are being fulfilled. They are also ways to incorporate shipping apps into your back end you can cut down the shipping process. These apps allow you to print labels for the products that people order, so you just have to package your product and take it to the store. However, if you want to customize everything for your site there is another way.

The next way, if you have a lot of money and you do not mind customizing your site, is to build a site from scratch. You will hire a graphic designer and a coder and let them design everything. They will build the site from scratch using code. If you have a graphic designer who can code, that's even better. This method can be expensive, but it lets you have all the features that you want on your website. The most difficult part will be to find a designer that can design the site according to your specifications. Of course, you want to look inside job boards like freelancer or fiverr.com or upwork.com to see if you can find the designer. You can also find designers that will use WordPress to design a website for you.

You just want to make sure that you have some type of documentation and place for confidentiality reasons and make sure you have great communication in your working relationship. Some people like to accept your payment, without doing your work. So make sure that you have specific guidelines about when they are getting paid. This option is definitely for more advanced people, and you may spend more money up front, but in the long term, it may help you save more money if your site becomes very popular and you start having higher volume. The more places you are the more chances you have to make more money. So you want to also consider being on sites like Etsy, eBay, and Amazon. These sites have a fee per sale model. There are many different options you can use to sell your products. You just have to think about your short-term and long-term goals in order to choose the one that fits the idea that you are trying to do.

Every year you will want to evaluate your website. As you make more money, you may even consider hiring a business coach to look at your website, especially one that specializes in e-commerce. A business coach can point out to you areas of opportunity to improve sales just based on your website. They can help you find where you need to create a sense of urgency that will increase sales. They will also know which plugins that you can add that will improve the overall customer's purchase when they come to your website. They may be expensive, so this is a step you want to take when you definitely have more money. If you have enough money upfront, do not be afraid to invest in yourself. They can definitely help.

When your website is created do not forget to have a frequently asked questions page to answer questions about shipping and other pressing issues. Also, make sure you have a way for people to contact you as well. This is information that people want to know. If they are able to easily look on your website and find it, that will save you a lot of time.

CHAPTER 7

FINDING YOUR PERFECT MANUFACTURER

Finding a good manufacture is so important. It is the link between creating your creations for one person to helping your creations spread to the masses. Manufacturers can help you create whatever you want whether it is sportswear, jackets, rain coats, lingerie, men's clothes, women's clothes, outdoor wear, street wear, high fashion, pajamas, luggage, or anything that you can think of to bring to life. In the past, finding manufacturers was a very difficult process. Thankfully today with the advent of the internet and apps that are disrupting the manufacturing industry, it is a lot easier to find manufacturers and deal with them directly. You no longer have to be a huge business to take advantage of the benefits of using a manufacturer. You also no longer have to live in an area where there are manufacturers or wholesale districts nearby. The internet has made the world a lot smaller and now is your time to take advantage of it. This chapter will discuss all the ways of finding the manufacturers to help you make large orders of your clothing.

The first way to find a manufacturer is to visit the wholesale districts in your area. Get to know the business owners and be nice to them. They will be able to help you find information that's not available online since they are on the ground. Introduce yourself and always try to be polite to them. You can give them your business card, or even a follow them on Instagram. When you are positioning who you are, always let them know that you are willing to help them with whatever they may need. People are more open to connecting if you come with the benefits you can offer them versus what you can gain from them. The manufacturers will also offer to be able to offer some advice that can help you see what the latest trends are in the area. You can also host a happy hour or networking for other small clothing companies in the area so you can exchange tips and information if you aren't a near a lot of manufacturers. If you are near manufacturers, you can ask them to come to the happy hour. The more you can engage with people in the industry who are actually doing what you want to do, you can learn from them. Network, network, network. If you are friendly with your local manufacturers, they will help you build inside connections in the business. Whatever you do, do not burn bridges. Always be polite because you never know who you are going to meet. When you do engage with these companies or other business owners, you can ask them a few questions.

- Where do you find your clothing from?
- Are you buying wholesale or manufacturing your clothes yourself?
- Are you using blank companies that are local or are the blanks shipped in from out of the country?
- What companies should you avoid?

- What companies should I use?

Connecting with others will help you find manufacturers easier. When you have identified who your manufacturer is going to be, start off the relationship by making a small order. If possible, order 2 sizes for each design you have. Then you can work your way up to a decent order of 45 pieces of one order. This is called a slow build up. By doing it this way, you can meet market demand and scan to find out what your customer like. That way you can always design things that people like and that you know will sell. Once you have found the manufacturer you want to use, it is time to ask a few questions.

Cut and Sew Manufacturers

If you can, try to find local manufactures for cut and sew designs as well. If you cannot find a local manufacturer, at least find one in the same country that you are in. Starting off, you do not want to outsource directly to China for a few reasons.

For a beginner, it is very hard to do, and you will waste a lot of money because things get lost in translation. Most of the manufacturers do not speak English. There are also different etiquette rules with foreign manufactures. Sometimes they may say something that is totally different than what you are expecting. So, starting off, try to avoid it to save money and confusion.

The next reason you want to avoid overseas manufacturers is that they have a different measuring system. Their sizes are not the same; thus, when you place a big order, you can be bitterly surprised when it does not come out the way you expected. Chinese sizes are often smaller than western sizes. If your target demographic is on the smaller end, you may consider doing business with a Chinese manufacturer for smaller sizes at a later date. However, you will have to have top-notch communication and be more experiences. This step is definitely not for the beginner and even advanced clothiers will not take this step.

Another reason to avoid overseas manufacturers is because you can't meet them face-to-face. When you are doing such an intricate process, it is best to meet the manufacturer face-to-face to make sure you are on the same page.

If this is your first time finding a manufacturer, then it would be hard learning the ropes to an unfamiliar industry and on top of that, it will be even more difficult if you have no one to speak your language to help you.

The next important reason to avoid jumping into relationships with an overseas manufacturer is that it will take forever for you to send samples back and forth. If the order is wrong, it will take forever for the correction to be fixed, and you won't get refunded. Not to mention, it may take longer if any arise when you are dealing with customs. Try to stay local.

Once you have identified the manufacturers that you want to use, now is the time to contact them. When you contact them, start off with a simple email. That way you can email multiple manufacturers on the phone, and you won't spend a lot of time playing phone tag. The simple email should include a few questions.

- What is your minimum order requirement?

- What is the cost for how much for what you want to order?
- What is your turnover time? Most manufacturers can give you a turnover time of 4 weeks usually.
- Give them a brief idea of what you want to do and ask do they think it is possible.
- Ask about shipping and how to handle delays?
- What happens if the order isn't right? Will you be refunded?

For cut and sew and blank manufacturers, you will also need to send them fabric, designs, schedules, logos, hang tags, and contracts. If you are going to order a small bag of clothes from them, make sure that your pricing covers your expenses. This will ensure that you are making back your money and have some extra to reinvest back into your brand. If you are creating a more luxurious, be sure to harp upon that it is one 0f kind of exclusive or has limited supplies to create a sense or urgency and justify the higher price. When you set your pricing, make sure that you are setting a price that's fair for you and your customers. Do not underprice yourself because if you are not making enough profit, you can start to resent your business. Also, if you start off at a lower price, do not be afraid to raise your rates at any time. On your website, be sure to have a notice that prices can change at any time. When dealing with cut and sew manufacturers, you have to also be mindful of changes and materials due to business policies for any other factors. One thing is for certain, as long as you have a quality product, people do not mind paying the price for it. Do not begin by cutting yourself out the game.

The secret to manufacturing is to remember this. The production and quality of the products are based on what you ask for and what you are willing to pay. Once you are more established, using an overseas manufacturer is not a bad option, but you need to learn the ropes for. Chinese manufactures will only give you what you pay for so you will need to know what you are asking for. When you are ready to up the ante and take your business to the other level and deal with Chinese manufacturers, you will learn that everything in China isn't social irresponsible.

As long as your sample is right and they are working off the right sample, everything can turn out well. Some people even like to visit the manufacturers in person to form a relationship with them. Try to be respectful in your dealings with your manufacturers. Respect, patience, and communication can go a long way. Also, do not be afraid to call out the manufacturer when you think they are being unfair. They may feign ignorance, but make sure that you are making your point with proof and make it fairly. Bargain with the manufacturer until you are able to get the deal that you want. If not, do not be afraid to move on.

Just remember before working with a manufacturer try to communicate with the manufacturers first. The best way to ease into a relationship with the manufacturer is by sending emails. Then you can see who was responding and gauge the quality of the answers. If this seems acceptable, then you can order a sample and then gauge the sample that they send you. If the sample isn't the best product, it is a red flag because the sample is what is going to be replicated. If it is a poor sample, go ahead and find another manufacturer. Keep using this template until you are able to find what you are looking for.

When you finally do get your sample, make sure that your quality assurance is strict. Quality assurance is just the fancy name for making sure that your products have the quality that you need. Try to get a sample at every phase of the design to ensure that it is coming out with the highest qualify. Even if it is a one-person quality assurance team, make sure you check the quality no matter if it is coming from an overseas or a domestic manufacturer. Sometimes cut and sew manufactures are hard to work with because they do not want to do small orders. They would rather have their machines set up once to produce lots of orders rather than a small amount. If you run into a cut and sew manufacturer that's giving you a hard time, you can keep looking and find one that does not mind working with a lower amount of minimal orders. When you do send your information for samples, make sure that you are sending vector base designs for logos and graphic design so you can get the highest quality possible. One of the best websites to find manufacturers is to use sites like Maker's Row or Sewport. A lot of these manufacturers often take small minimum orders since they are working with small businesses.

Blank Manufacturers

It can be much easier to work with a blank manufacturer after you do your initial research. Just like working with a cut and sew manufacturer, you want to send them an email, too, with similar questions. After you send an email and find a company you are willing to work with, you can then send the blanks to the manufacturer who will complete the rest of the process. Remember when you are working with a blank manufacturer, you have to buy the accessories that you want added to your materials. So be sure to inquire with your manufacturer the best way to do this. An example of a blank manufacturer is Thrasher Tees. They are able to handle a larger volume of orders because they are using blanks to scale their products and offer cheaper prices for their customers. Once you have found your blank manufacturer, you also want to see if they will relabel your products. Relabeling products just means that you are going to swap out the blanks brand information with yours. One of the easiest ways to do that is with labels. You can find any printing company in order to print your labels to make this process go easier. Some of the most popular blank Manufacturing companies:

- Apliiq
- https://mysimplicated.com/
- https://dadsewinghouse.com/
- HSApperal

You can also type in apparel manufacturers on Google to find more blank manufacturers that make the specific type of clothing that you are trying to make. Do not take for granted the benefits of using online clothing forums. When you Google information regarding blank manufacturers, do not be afraid to go deep into your search and look past the first page results. You can even use different search engines, like FireFox or other web browsers, in order to see what different results will appear. When you go deep into the search results, you may be able to find pages that contain forums. These forums often have excellent advice that is not found in regular search results. When you are researching any product, do not be afraid to use different web browsers. You may be surprised at the results you find.

Now if you are interested in using overseas manufacturers after you have a little more experience, AliExpress isn't that bad. However, for the best results, you may want to check out Alibaba. Alibaba a slightly higher quality than AliExpress and they are used to build dealing with businesses more. The Factory Confirmed by Sourcify is a great tool to use if you do not want to research Alibaba manually. This is a Chrome extension, and it is free. However, you can find a manufacturer with a manual process by researching and emailing.

- The first thing you want to do is go to the Ali Baba site. Create an account.
- Second, set the filters to place a minimum order with a volume less than 20 units.
- Do not be overly concerned about the pictures. It is just showing that the manufacturer is good at the manufacturing that they are using.
- Third, after you find a company that you want, email them. Send a well thought out message as to your brand, who you are, what country you are from, and what you want. Notice how well they respond, and how quickly they respond. Ask them about any other companies that they work with as well to

see if you need to see the quality of what they've done. Look for spelling errors and proper grammar. If they do not have a good translator then it will be a lot harder to communicate with them. So, if there English is bad then move on to the next one.

- Fourth, copy and paste the message to everyone with the minimum order of the clothing you need. Most manufactures are going to bargain with you to get your minimum order up. Do not be surprised. Stick to the original minimum order and do not feel pressure to go higher.
- Fifth, if some manufactures respond, ask them a bunch of questions. Listen to their answers but continue to do your own research. Look at their website through their Alibaba page. Through Alibaba, you can check their company profile. If they are a verified Business, check their reviews. Most importantly check their trade assurance. If the manufacturer has only been around for a year, it might be a little risky to work with them. However, if they been around for eight years or more, you are in the clear. This will narrow your search down to find out who will be the best to work with and who won't scam you.
- Sixth- You want to go back and forth with them to get a sample of your desired clothing. You will have to pay for the sample. And you can pay a little less if you decide not to ship it and if they can take a picture of it. However, you cannot feel the clothing, so it is better to pay the extra $50 or so to ship it.

- Seventh- After the sample process, you will have to be very clear and exact with your placement and sizing of your logos. Everything must be explained exactly how you want it.
- Eight- If production times are taking longer than expected, then keep in communication. Human error is common in this method and constant communication is a good thing and make the experience much better.

And that's how you get overseas manufacture with minimum orders of ten pieces per design! Be prepared to communicate well and keep a sense of humor about the entire process. This isn't a fool proof way, things may and will happen but it the prices are all worth it.

Always compare the prices of local manufactures and overseas to see which one is better. Thankfully, there a lot of different ways that you can manufacture your work. You just have to find what's ideal for you and your brand. If you think you found the best deal, look one more time. Oftentimes, we find that amazing deal after just one more try. Even when you work with the manufacturer, keep looking because you may be able to find other manufacturers at lower prices which will cause your manufacture to lower their prices in order to continue working with you. Use your research to your advantage.

CHAPTER 8

SMART MARKETING 101

Once your clothes are in the process of being created, you will want to start marketing. You do not want to wait until your clothes are finished to start marketing. Marketing is the long-term process and you can start building excitement from for your clothing idea from the beginning to create more intense marketing buzz. You should get into the habit of doing marketing every day. The sooner you can begin marketing, the better. This chapter will look at the best ways you can market your clothing company if you are just getting started. We will focus on social media, with an emphasis on social media, and guerilla marketing.

Instagram is going to be a very popular way to market your clothing company since it is a visual-heavy social media platform. If you want to be taking seriously as a clothing company, you definitely want to have an Instagram. Even if you have no experience with marketing, this chapter will help. One of the easiest ways to figure out how to market your brand is for you to look at other companies and see what they are doing. What does their Instagram look like? Are they using certain colors or are they focused more on stories? Are they just posting information without using color schemes or does it seem to have a method to their posting? It is important to think about what you want your imaging to look like on Instagram and make sure that it falls into your brand. You can begin marketing even if you do not have a name yet by engaging followers. You can ask them what's the best name that you can use for your business. You can also build engagement with your follower asking for their input about the colors you going to use on the website or even logo designs. This will get people excited about what you are trying to do. When you finally have your brand assets, make sure that your logo is prominent on your Instagram page and have a link to your site and post your business' hashtag, as well.

When you are using social media, try to create an identity that you want your business to be identified across every marketing efforts you use. Create a manual outlining your identity and purpose. This manual is also called a brand book. This will help you to keep your marketing efforts stay consistent as you grow. As more people are added to your team, it will help them know what's appropriate to post and what's not appropriate. This brand book may change, but it is good to have it in case you need to let anyone else run your social media. Feel free to modify this document to encapsulate what your most successful branding efforts are. Once you create the document, you can get a graphic designer to design it and have it as an official document. Some things you can include in the brand book are as follows:

The first thing you want is an 'About the brand' section. This will have what the mission, target audience, and overall values of the brand are. It can be short or long. It just depends on how detailed you want it to be. After the 'About the brand' section, you will want to add in the visual guidelines.

Communications guidelines:

Language - What language will you use in your brand's communications?

Readability – Will you use short or long sentences?

Grammar and formatting: Will you use shorthand or stick to formal conventions?

Style - Will you use jargon, formal, slang, or relaxed language?

Email -What will your email signature's look like?

Copy- What is actually being said and how it is being said.

Visual guidelines include:

Tagline - Where will you place it?

Colors – What are the primary and secondary colors?

Other graphics - What will those other graphics look like? Will they have a certain texture or pattern?

Photography – What type of photography is acceptable to use?

Brandmark – Where will you use it and when? Also, what color or style will it be?

Logo – What is the appropriate way to use your logo? What size, color, and placement is appropriate? What would be considered a misuse of the logo?

Editorial style guide – What is the official formatting and structure for blog posts?

Typography –What is considered the standard and appropriate fonts in body text and headlines of official communication?

Social media – What is the official social media schedule?

Once you figure out your style guide, it is time to get to posting.

The first place you want to have a presence is Instagram. Instagram is important. You've got to have it. Instagram is probably the most important marketing platform for your brand in this era and one of the easiest to use. When you do start with Instagram, you can post pictures with your clothes with the models in a certain setting that compliments your brand. For example, if your vibe is laid back. You can have people chilling on the beach. If your brand sells baby clothes, what better way to show that then have cute pictures of cute babies in your clothes. Post pictures that feel they can see themselves in. Making your content relevant and engaging allows other to begin to really understand what your brand does it goes a long way towards building brand awareness.

When using Instagram, make sure you are using stories - a lot! You can use them to update followers on designs, new lines that you are launching, photoshoots, and behind the scenes content. Again, make sure that your stories are relevant to your brand and the brand niche. Instagram can take a lot of time, so be patient and be consistent. If anyone engages with you, make sure you comment back. Do not mind following people who say kind words or reposting people who are wearing your brand. Before you post always think about how it relates to your brand. Is your post helping your brand move forward or is it not focused on your branding at all? Be very specific with your brand vibe because this is how your customer will relate to you. McDonald's is not going to post anything about vegetables and vegan because that's not what their brand is. Make sure what your posting relates directly to your brand. Branding is the constant visual aesthetic of your business. So, take your time and decide what method you want to use. Remember something doesn't work do not be afraid to change it. It is not a deal-breaker to change your mind.

If you want to build your followers quickly, consider always running a promotion. This will keep people interested in your Instagram page. You can also consider running ads on Instagram. If you can afford $2 to $5 a day for Instagram advertisements, do it. When you sign up to business. Instagram.com they will walk you through the steps of creating your Instagram business account. When you are up and running, be mindful of what your posting. You definitely do not want to post any random garbage. This can confuse the people who are fans of your brand as well as weaken your brand awareness. Within Instagram marketing you will be able to target people based on different factors such as interest and location. This is another reason it is important to have a customer avatar.

You just do not want to post your products all the time so it is important to switch up your posts. Try to change it up. If you run out of ideas or needs some ideas to help, here are a few Instagram ideas that you can post.

Behind the scene posts - People love to see what's going on behind the scenes. Behind the scenes, posts can show what your employees are doing or what you were doing to move the business forward like having meetings at a coffee shop. Behind the scenes, posts show that you not just a corporation, but that you are someone that has a dream and that you are going for it. You can also be funny and genuine. People can tell if you are faking or not. Let your personality show so people can relate to you.

Volunteering posts or stories - There is nothing that tugs at the heartstrings more than by posting ways that you are involved in the community. Show that your company is not just about profits. Show how you help out in the community. People will be interested in that and be willing to support.

Product creation posts -- This is always fascinating. When people understand how clothes are made, it makes the brand seems more personal and it adds more brand awareness.

Cross-promotion of other brands – Cross -promotion of other brands may seem counterintuitive, but it can be a good idea. If your brand look is good for people who like sitting in and writing in the coffee shop, why not partner with a coffee shop across the street? This way you both are promoted, and you form a relationship with another business in the process. When you made your brand identity, you created a lot of detailed questions about what your customer likes to do. Look at that brand identity questionnaire and then try to find connections that you can use with other brands.

Celebrating popular achievements – You have milestone posts that celebrate important achievements such as reaching 100 followers, or a thousand followers, or a million followers. You can also celebrate anything in between. Just be sure to show gratitude to your followers.

Giveaways - Giveaways are a fun way to engage your followers and get more followers. When you host a giveaway, make sure you have some type of incentive for the followers, whether they are tagging other people in your posts or using hashtags make sure that is getting your brand is getting out.

Discounts and promotions - Make sure that if you are offering promotions that they are in line with your business. You do not want to cut into your profit so do not underprice yourself. Some businesses do not offer discounts or promotions at all, and that's okay. You have to determine if you want to offer them or not. Just do not underprice your brand if you do.

Quotes - Inspirational quotes are always a fun way to engage your followers and to get people to follow you. Think about quotes that describe your business or the aesthetic of your business and you can use them.

Sneak peeks -Giving people exclusive content about things that are coming to the forefront that has not been released is another way to engage your followers. They know that if they aren't following you on Instagram, they are going to be out the loop so surprise your followers every now and then.

Repost Your Followers -This is a popular one to use because you do not have to do anything. You can simply repost someone else's information and inspirational caption about why this relates to your brand. Or you can simply post someone who bought your products and looks good in it. If other people can see that others are wearing your brands, it goes a long way to show your brand's relevance. An interesting idea is to send them a follow up email asking them to take a picture of them wearing it and send it in with the chance you will post a picture on their Instagram. It would be a fun thing for your customers to get some exposure and get free content by engaging your followers in hopes that they will want to do the same.

Whether your posting on Instagram or any social media, take advantage of hashtags so people can follow you easily. Use hashtags that your followers are using and make sure you have your business-branded hashtag in all your posts. This is just a hashtag specific to your posts. Also, in your captions of all social media posts have your followers doing something in your caption. Try to encourage your followers to share your content so you can get more information out about your business. You can also share other simple actions to do. That way your marketing efforts will be compounded instead of just posting pretty pictures with no actions given. Some action words that are good to in captions are…

- Use our hashtag
- Tell a friend
- Tag a friend
- Tell us what you think
- Enter our giveaway.

Be observant and watch how other businesses are using their captions and hashtags, and do not be afraid to take inspiration from that.

Another way to get the word out about your brand is if you work with influencers on Instagram. In the beginning you can work with influencers that have Instagram accounts ranging from 1,000 to 9,000 followers. Influencers at this size would love to get free clothes, and to be put on your page if you have a good following. They also love to get clothes in exchange for a post about your brand, but beware. You want to make sure that they are not buying their followers. When you see someone that has a sizable following, look at their pictures and see if they have some type of engagement on their posts. Do they have comments and likes or are their posts blank? The more engaged their followers are, the more engaged they will be about the post about your posts which can result in more sales.

Instagram is just one aspect of your sales funnel. A sales funnel is what you used to guide people to make a purchase for you. For example, if you post something on Instagram you ultimately drive them to your website to make a purchase. If you post a promotion on Instagram, your guiding them down your funnel with the photo so they will buy from you. Sales are what matters at the end of the day so make sure the content your posting is helping you make sales.

Instagram's sister company Facebook is also another valuable way to market your business. With over a billion people using the platform, you are sure to find someone to like your brand. Similar to Instagram you can come up with your social media posts. You can also connect your Facebook account to your Instagram account and whatever posts on your Instagram will also post on your Facebook automatically. If you do not have a lot of time, that will be the easiest route. However, if you have different content on different platforms, that diversifies your brand and make sure that people are tuned in with you on every social media platform. Facebook ads are also very effective. Similar to Instagram ads, you can run ad every day and your targeting size will be based on how much you are willing to pay a day. Business.Facebook.com is the website to go to start your Facebook ads. Facebook ads are really easy to get off the ground, and there are lots of tutorials on YouTube that can show you how to use them. This is not a Facebook ads book but this is an aspect of marketing that is very useful. The main thing when using Facebook ads to make sure that you are advertising to people who you know will resonate with your brand. That way you are not wasting money attracting people that have no idea who you are.

You also will want to continue to find other brands, accounts, people that capture your brand's values or are similar to the vibe of your brand. Comment, follow and message them across all social media platforms. This will help you to build relationships and help your business thrive. You do not have to follow millions of people every day, but make a goal to maybe like, comment, or follow 5 people a day. You can unfollow them later if they don't reciprocate interest. Whatever you decide, be consistent and you will watch your following grow. The more exposure you have the better. So do not just limit yourself to Instagram or Facebook. You can use Pinterest, Tumblr, or whatever social media platform is best for you. However, you want to separate your marketing efforts when you are evaluating where you get the most engagement. That way you can know which items are working for you and what things are not working for you. For example, if you noticed that most of your sales come from Instagram, you would want to spend more time on Instagram since that is bringing more sales for you. Anytime you have a sale, you can ask people where they heard about you. You will then realize where your marketing efforts are best spent.

What you decide what social media platforms you want to be on, it can be more than Instagram and Facebook, you will want to create a social media posting schedule. This helps you to stay organized, and have your content made in advance. It will also help you to outsource your social media posting to a virtual assistant if necessary. When you are creating the social media schedule, you can brainstorm different ideas of what you would like to post about. For example, every Monday it can be something related to your brand. Then on Tuesday maybe you can post people that are wearing your clothing. On Wednesday it can be another discount day. And you continue to create content every day until your social media is planned.

Depending on which platform you are using, you can find a way to upload posts in advance. That way the part work of posting is already done, and you just have to monitor and respond to the comment when the post goes out. Hootsuite and Buffer are popular software tools that allow you to schedule your posts in advance. If you need help managing your Instagram, you can investigate bots and Instagram managing services. To create professional-looking post, Canva is a great, free resource to use. With Canva, there are professional templates already created that you could edit to fit your colors. Then you just download the posts and then upload them. You can even create posts from scratch if necessary. Every month evaluate the types of post that are popular and then create those posts over again. When you post about certain topics, you will see more likes and comments. If so, continue to post those types of posts. If you do not see any type of engagement for a certain post, you can consider changing what you post. The social media plan is not set in stone and it is a way to make your life easier while you handle other aspects of your business. If you do decide to outsource this work to someone else, you can look at websites such as upwork.com or fiber.com to find a virtual assistant that specializes in social media. Of course, the more you post on Instagram or any social media platform, the more engaged your followers will be. However, sometimes you do not have time to do that. So, start off being consistent even if it is just one post a day and then grow from there. If you start off doing 10 posts a day, people are going to expect that. You can always start small and grow a little bit. That's where using bots and having assistance with your social media is helpful. You can also look for interns, like college students or relatives, who are looking to work with a growing brand to help manage your social media. Use what you have.

You also want to incorporate some form of email marketing. Ask for customer's emails in exchange for a discount coupon or a special gift if they sign up. That way when they sign up, you always have a way to tell people about your brand. Popular email marketing systems include MailChimp, which is free up to 2,000 people, and Aweber which has a month-long free trial. An email list is very important. In case Instagram was to ever shut down your account, you will still have the emails of people who are your followers and you do not have to start from scratch. It is also important to have your own website, that way if Instagram shut you down you still have property where people engage with your brand. When you are running promotions on your social media, be sure that some of those promotions have incentives for people who give you their email. Another great and easy way to get people's emails is when you are launching your website. You can have a website in a countdown timer on your website and a place for them to give you your email when it launches. Having email is also important because you can send them reminder emails in case they were going to buy something from you but forgot. Shopify has this feature build in already.

Another important form of marketing that you can use is guerrilla marketing. Guerrilla marketing is using non-traditional marketing ways or more passive ways to help you sell your product. They are often low-cost as well and creative. One example guerrilla marketing is to have a sticker or other merchandise like lighters, grocery bags, pencils, or pens that have your branding design. That way when people see your brand, they may look it up. You can share this type of merch to make sure your brand is always advertised. Another effective way to advertise your business is through your email signature. Make sure you have your brand's information in your email signature and that info will go out to everyone that you email. This helps them remember your brand. You also do not want to forget to ask your friends and family members to market for you. Most people will do it for free because they believe in you and your product. On the day of lunch or even occasionally, you can get them to post on their social media or repost your post on your businesses Instagram page. That way information about your product is being spread by multiple people. To take this up a notch you can make a list of all your friends, associates and family members that have a social media presence and then politely ask them to share information. Most people will love to do so. You can even stagger the times that they post so it won't be all at one time. This ensures that your information is being spread at different times in a strategic fashion. Additionally, you can take advantage of the direct sales method of selling and focus on the relationships that you have. You can decide to host clothing parties for your clothing line. This way you are having fun and selling in a social setting. Most people do not mind coming to a party to buy. You can also add in parks for people who purchase a piece of clothing before they get there. Add extra perks for those people who purchase more than one piece of clothing. Of course, you want to set the atmosphere with music and have food and drinks. Whatever you do, make sure that the party atmosphere matches your brand.

You also will want to join your local Chamber of Commerce. This step may cost a small fee, and it may not, but it is very effective. Tapping into your local market can help your business thrive. When you are a member of your chamber of commerce. They will do everything they can to see you succeed. They often have networking events and workshops that you can take advantage of that will help your business grow. If you are a minority, you will also want to consider joining the minority Chamber of Commerce in your city. Joining a Chamber of Commerce is the best kept secret to starting your own online business. Everyone has to wear clothes, and they will be a great way to advertise your business through word-of-mouth. You also will be able to join a community of entrepreneurs that all deal with common business problems. You will be able to talk with them and figure out how to navigate issues that you are having that all businesses experience. another way to find a community of entrepreneurs to connect with would be to use Craigslist, or social gathering sites like meetup.com. They often have entrepreneur groups that you can join. Some of these groups even require that you have referrals every month. If there is not such a gathering in your community, you may want to consider starting one. Starting a networking group will be a great way to spread the word about your business as well as forming a community of entrepreneurs.

There are a few other tips to keep in mind when marketing. You can have birthday promotions to reward people for being loyal to you. You can give them small gifts, coupons, or discounts. This goes a long way into building your brand awareness. You will also want to have a launch party. You can take footage of it and invite people. You can also send out press releases, so people know to come. And after you launch, remember to keep marketing. Do a little bit every day so you are not overwhelmed. Come up with a name for people who wear your clothing and create a Facebook group or address them on your Instagram posts. This helps people feel special and soon everyone will want to wear what you are selling. You can also have gift guides all year long and describe cool ways to wear your clothing. You can also post different blog posts to engage people while providing them with value. Try to maintain integrity and build your brand the hard way. This will pay off better in the long run.

To take your marketing efforts to another level, you can even think about hiring a sales representative. Sales are the lifeline of your both of your business so if you have someone that is a master at sales then you can definitely grow your business. However, you want to make sure that the perks are worth it for the sales representative. Once you know how much money on advertisements that you had to spend in order to get a customer, you will know how to scale easily. You want to make sure you are making note of how many followers you have month by month so you can see your growth. You can also see if the growth with your followers is corresponding to sales. Remember, marketing is all about sales. You may be doing something that is fun and enjoyable with takes a lot of time but is resulting in no sales. In that case, you may want to pivot and refocus your efforts.

Just like every other aspect of your business as you are beginning your enterprise, you want to find ways to keep costs low. Try to take advantage of word-of-mouth marketing and guerrilla marketing before you go into your paid options. However, do not be afraid of paid advertisement. It is an important part of your business. Start off small with your paid advertisements and then scale once an advertisement begins to get a lot of sales. As you are running your advertisements, continue to learn the best practices about advertisements and marketing. That way you can ensure that you are getting the most bang for your buck. Remember a lot of social media platforms change their algorithms often so make sure that you are staying up to date with the latest trends. Continue to research and learn about marketing. Like a lot of things in business, observation is one of the best tools you can use. Do not mind looking and swiping what works for other people. Once you add your own touch to it, the content will be brand-new. Use them as inspiration if you see a successful and watch the dollars come rolling in.

CHAPTER 9

ORDER FULFILLMENT CRASH COURSE

After your brilliant marketing efforts are successful, you will have to fulfill the orders. Order fulfillment is the process of receiving the orders that were placed on your website, packaging them and shipping them out to the customer. You can either do the fulfillment yourself or you can hire an order fulfillment company to do it for you. There are pros and cons to each one. Your fulfillment needs will change over time so do not feel like you are locked in to one method. The more orders you began to sell, the more the order fulfillment method will change to make sure that you are getting the most cost-effective deals. When you are using print-on-demand, the orders are filled by another company. So, you do not have to touch the actual inventory. They handle everything for you. If you do not go to print-on-demand route, you must fulfill the orders yourself. There are a few things you must consider. There are different ways to do order fulfillment. You can do it in-house which means you store the inventory and you ship it out yourself. You can also do a third-party order fulfillment meaning that you send your inventory to a third party and they take care of the shipping. The next way to tackle order fulfillment is by using a hybrid approach where you can do a hybrid approach which combines a few different options. Before you begin selling, you have to map out a plan and go from there.

Order fulfillment is difficult because there are so many variables. It is difficult, but it is not impossible to do if you do diligent research. As you are preparing to ship your items, you need to consider the most cost-effective ways to ship. This will require you to do research to figure out the best way to ship your items. You also want to think about the type of experience that your customer will have when they get your package. Do you want them to have branded boxes that they open filled with lots of confetti and colored packing peanuts? Or are you ok with a less exciting unboxing? Whatever it is, you will want to think about the experience ahead of time so you can figure out a way to make it happen.

After you decide the type of experience you want the customer to have, you want to figure out what type of boxes or packaging you will use. Of course, the more environmentally friendly you are, the better. You also can save costs by using the smallest packaging possible. Choosing the packaging is a trial-and-error process so be sure to get samples of your packaging in different packages. That way you can see which option is most cost-effective and you can see what the customer is experiencing. While you want the packing to look pretty when the customer opens it, it is more important that the package and its contents be protected and safe. If there is a way to incorporate both at a cost-effective price, that's ideal. You do not want your clothing to be so tightly packaged that people find it difficult to open the package. So, try to be practical when choosing what type of packaging to use.

You can also check the calculators of certain carriers to see which one has the most effective rates depending on the weight and the packaging that you use. To take the packaging branding up a notch, you may want to add stickers, business cards, or even your branded packaging tape to be part of the unboxing experience. However, when you first start out, try to keep it as simple as possible so you can maximize your profits. If you want to ship from home, you might want to invest in a label printer as well as a digital scale. That way you can weigh packages at your home instead of having to go out to have your packages weighted at the carrier.

Once you figure out the packaging, the next thing you want to figure out is what carrier to use. Where you are shipping from and who your shipping to is going to be a great indicator of how much your shipping will cost. You also want to consider if you are going to have tracking and insurance on your packages. Both can be extra expenses. Costs can also change depending on if you are delivering to a business or residential environment. So be sure to include in your shipping policy on your website if you do not deliver to certain locations like PO Boxes.

In order to decide which carrier to use, you must figure out your shipping options for your site. One of the easiest drivers for sales is to have free shipping on your website. With this option, the shipping is calculated into the price already. However, do not inflate your prices too much because this will cause a competitor to be more appealing to the customer. Some eCommerce owners do not even try to make money from shipping. They try to cut shipping costs and make their profits in the price of their clothing. It just depends on what you think is best. You can also just add to your clothing price the cost of shipping, so you at least break even with shipping. You definitely do not want to eat shipping costs. When you start reaching a higher volume of sales, your shipping costs can add up quickly. You do not want to go in debt just because you did not cover shipping properly.

Another shipping strategy is to have free shipping after a certain dollar amount. This ensures that the transaction that every customer is using is high enough to account for free shipping. Other companies have a flat free shipping rate. After you figure out the shipping options, you can then figure out which carrier will be the most cost effective to use. Deciding on who you use to ship is dependent upon cost versus reliability. You have to decide if you do not mind paying a little bit extra to make sure the package is delivered in a timely fashion or if you do not mind waiting a little bit longer. You will also have to consider if you want to ship internationally or not.

Then after you actually ship the package you have to be concerned about returns and customer service. If you decide to tackle this by yourself, you can think about outsourcing help for customer service. You can find customer service reps by posting on indeed Freelancer, Upwork or even fiverr.com. One popular platform you can use to handle customer service request is Freshdesk.com. Freshdesk gives you the option to answer emails or even contact by phone. People love to ask questions, so try to cut down questions they may have by having your policies clearly listed on your website. In this policy section, you can have them listed separately or in your frequently asked questions sections. If you let people know that there will be no returns, and then they will be aware and that may save you some time. Think of the most common questions people may have about your clothing. Those questions can be about the material that you use, the way your clothing is created, is it sustainable, is it ethically responsible, is it eco-friendly? Think of all the popular questions people may ask and put it in that section. Hopefully, they can save you some time and respond to customers. Unfortunately, not everyone reads and you still will get some questions. By having your policies listed on your website, you will be able to answer a lot of the request easily and let disgruntled customers know that the information was provided at the time of purchase. If you can have a way for customers to check their own shipping, that will also save you a lot of time. If you decide to use Shopify, there is a way for you to connect an app that allows people to enter in their tracking number so they can track the information themselves.

Oftentimes depending on what shipping carrier you use, once it leaves your hands it is out of your control. The only thing you can do is refer them to the shipping company. However, you do need to think of a policy to address what's going to happen if packages get lost in the mail or if customers did not receive their packages. You must decide what you think is fair and put that in the policy as well. Just like everything in this business, before you select a carrier make sure that you do plenty of research.

Another important part of order fulfillment that you want to consider is where you will keep your inventory if you are not doing print-on-demand. If you do not have a huge batch of inventory, you can possibly keep the inventory in a spare room in your house or in the garage. However, you want to watch out for smells in whatever room you keep the inventory, so the clothing will not absorb unpleasant smells. Then you will have to figure out a system to package up the goods when it is time to ship them out. You can buy packaging in bulk use a shipping software to print off the label. You can either decide to use FedEx or the US Postal Office. They oftentimes have free packaging, so you do not have to spend money on packaging. This will prevent you from having a branded experience, but it will allow you to save a lot of money. If you do it yourself, you can look into hiring relatives or young teens who do not mind helping you pack your packages. However, do not fall into the trap of just hiring someone just because they are cheaper. Sometimes you need to pay a little bit extra to make sure that your needs are being met. After the goods are packaged, you have to decide if you are going to talk about all the packages to the carrier or set up a delivery. You can also decide to store the inventory in a separate warehouse and ship from the warehouse. Mind you, if you do store the information in the separate warehouse, they may charge you a warehouse fee to store the product.

If you do decide to fulfill your orders, you can create a system using an Excel sheet and or pen and paper to figure out how to track your orders. However, there are lots of software in the eCommerce space that helps manage your order fulfillment. They allow you to see when the order was placed, if the order has been fulfilled, and if it has been shipped yet. This organization helps you in case the customer ever has a question about their package. If you do not want to do this manually by hand, you can use lots of software out there. Many of these programs incorporate into e-commerce stores like Shopify or Big Cartel or even a WordPress site. If you do build your site from scratch, you can incorporate it into that website by using a certain cold. Common order fulfillment software are ShipStation, EasyPost, Shippit, EasyShip - good for customers that do a lot of shipping internationally.

If you do not want to deal with any fulfillment responsibilities, you can hire a third-party fulfillment service. You just ship your inventory to them, and then they charge you a processing fee to store, pack and ship your inventory. Make sure that you are aware of all the fees that are into considering when you use a fulfillment service and adjust your prices accordingly. When you have done research, reach out to the fulfillment company and see what they do. You also want to see if they process returns or not. You can also ask questions to see how they handle heavy volume. You can see if they are willing to add your branding to packaging and if that will have an extra cost. You can also see if they have any experience shipping similar items. Then get the info to those companies and talk to them yourself. That way you can decide if you want to go with that company or not.

Best Practices

If you are handling orders yourself, you want to investigate issues with shipping as soon as they occur. As soon as the customer reports that an issue happens with their package, you do the work of hard to figure out what's going on. Take the matter in to your own hands and make sure that information was entered correctly and that you've done all that you can do and then report back promptly to the customer.

Be aware of international shipping issues as well as domestic shipping issues. The more you are prepared for what's going on the better. This way people will not be confused about issues that may happen because of customs. Some people do not offer international shipping because it is just too difficult, and they do not want the headache. This is something you should consider. However, just know that if you do not offer international shipping, you do leave some money on the table. Take the time to do the research upfront and to make maximum profit.

Take responsibility even if it is not your fault. This isn't always popular or fun, but people feel better if they know that someone is handling their issue. If you play the blame game, it does not leave a good taste in the customer's mouth or help them feel confident in your ability.

Many businesses have relationships with different carriers depending on where they are going to ship their items. Smaller packages normally work better with the United States Postal Service and they even have tracking. However, try to you figure out which carrier is best for you, and try to take advantage of their discounts for being a loyal customer.

Let customers know that when they order the product by a certain time then the order will be shipped on the same day. If it is not ordered by a cut-off time, the order will be shipped the next day. This helps people that have an expectation when their order will be delivered. It also creates a sense of urgency that can cause them to purchase sooner rather than later. Lastly, it gives you some breather time, so you do not feel pressured to always package products to ship.

As much as you can, try to let the customer know when their package is going to arrive. If you let them know ahead of a time, they can expect it. However, make them aware of delays because of holidays or the weekends. Also, clearly specify the difference between a business day in a regular day. That way they won't be confused about when to expect their package. The more details you can give them, the better expectation the customer will have and the better experience they will have.

Always under-promise but over-deliver. People are not patient. So, make sure you give plenty of time so they can check the shipping themselves. Also, give them a shipping number so they can check their tracking themselves without having to continue with login or contact you about information.

See if your fulfillment center also does customer service for order fulfillment to save you even more time. They may respond to customer's request about refunds or lost packages. See if they do that. If not, you may be able to negotiate this service. When you are looking into order fulfillment, consider the customer service aspect. Customer service is one aspect that can make or break your brand. We all know brands that people hate to contact and their sales suffer as a result. If a company is known for great customer service, they will often have loyal fans who do not mind paying whatever price they ask. Establish a culture of excellent customer service from the aspect and you should be the person that starts that culture by your actions. As you grow, your employees will catch on and do the same.

Order fulfillment can be a headache if you are not organized. But once you figure out how to handle it. It is a piece of cake. You can play around with different systems until you figure out which one works best for you and your business. Whichever option you choose, try to keep costs as low as possible. Then you can upgrade to different options that are fancy your once you bring in more profit. You do not want to kill your business with your shipping cost. This is a cost that cannot be avoided, but it does not have to eat all your profits.

CHAPTER 10

MONEY, MONEY, MONEY, MONEY

You may want to start your own clothing company for warm and fuzzy reasons, but at the end of the day you are a business and your main goal is to make money. Money is what will allow you to continue to stay in business or to end your business. The chapter will discuss all things money and give you an idea of what you need to get started. The more capital you have initially is going to be more helpful, but do not think that if you do not have any money you still can't succeed. Having limited monetary resources can sometimes be a good thing. The lack of money causes you to become more creative in your solutions. We're going to base our suggestions on how to start your business if you have Capital between $600 and $700. Let's begin.

When you first start your clothing company there are some things that you just cannot skimp on. You want to make sure that you have a quality product. You need to have your own domain name, and you need to buy shipping supplies initially. Not just a shipping supplies, but you also need money to ship your items as well. So about how much is it going to cost you ask? This is where you must do your research and shop around for the best prices.

Product- Depending on your product, you can determine how much it will be based on if you are using print-on-demand, blanks, or a cut and sew method. Consider if you can spend less by placing a larger order. You can also see if they offer discounts for slight differences in the quality of clothing that most customers will not even notice.

A website domain can be as cheap as a dollar or more expensive if you want to buy it from someone else. Your website domain varies depending on the name that you want to use. But a simple.com website can run you about 10 bucks if the domain name is not on sale. After the initial purchase, there will be a small few to keep your domain name every year. That price will be given to you once you buy the domain name, but it is usually around the same price that you pay for your domain name.

If you are using a hosted website like Shopify, you have to account for the monthly fees to keep that going. You can just point your domain to the website. If you go in for a WordPress option, you do not have to pay a monthly fee to keep the website going but you do have to pay for an SSL certificate. That price varies depending on where you buy it from, but that can be anywhere from 25 to 50 bucks.

Shipping supplies -A bulk of the capital is going to be your shipping supplies. You want to try to buy those in bulk. You want to buy boxes, envelopes, or packing peanuts. You can decide if you want customized labels or not. Starting off, you can start to write your labels by hand. Then you can buy other branded merch, like your stickers, packaging tape, confetti or packing peanuts. Try to cut your shipping costs down as much as possible. Common places for people to look for shipping deals can be eSupplyStore, Uline, ValueMailers, Fast-

Pack, and eSupplyStore. Mind you, if you are using a carrier like UPS FedEx or the United States Postal Office, they often offer free packaging. Hence, you may save by using their packaging and as you make more money, then invest in branded packaging.

For the rest of your funds, use it to ship your items. Try to see what discounts the carriers have. It also may be important to create and use a business account to get further discounts. If you know anyone with military discounts who do not mind sharing with you, take advantage of that as well.

Pricing

When you are pricing your items consider the profit margin. You want to have around $20 is profit that will cover your shipping, your website subscription, and profit. Remember, you determine pricing. People will pay what you require if they see the benefit in it. Do not feel like you have to underprice yourself, but also do not feel like you have to over price yourself. Comparing your product to other people is good, but you have to figure out the best price for you to make sure you are making the profit that you want that will cover your expenses and leave money for a profit that you are ok with. It is important to have a pre-launch order. That way the money can serve as further capital for your business. To do a pre-launch, you can offer you products at a discounted price for the people who are interested.

The Bank Account Issue

It is important to have a separate business account. SERIOUSLY. This will save you a lot of headache in the long run. Keep the money you make in that account and reinvest. Continue to reinvest the money in your bank account for as long as you can. Take of bank offers that want to attract new business customers. You can also see if you can get a PayPal business account that consists of extras perks. Also, smartly invest that money that you make. For example, if you have the change to buy something in bulk, try to take advantage of that instead of doing something that you do not necessarily need at the moment. The only way to make money is to invest money. There is no getting without giving so you are going to have to give something up. Once you have money to invest, try to buy more product or to upgrade your packaging or have a better website experience. Only you can determine the best use of the money. Figure it out and do that. Some people do not like to touch their money at all. They only reinvest if for a few months or years. You can set a goal to not spend the money until until you reach a certain profit margin. Remember the name of the game is to keep costs low and sell high.

To Take Money Or Not To Take Money

At some point, once your business is up and running, you may have to decide if you want to take outside money or not. You also may have to decide if you want to crowdfund to raise the extra cost. The good thing about starting your business is that it shows you are willing to put in the work. People are more willing to invest with people who are working on their business rather than sitting back and talking. When you start your business, try to keep costs as low as possible so you can try to avoid taking outside money. This helps you to maintain control over your brand. However, if you realize that your business can be more successful by taking money, there are a few different ways you can get it.

The first way is to get a loan from a bank if you have good credit. Of course, taking a loan out it is not ideal, but it is an option. You can see if friends and family members will give you a loan as another option. nowadays, you can find many pitch competitions where you can pitch your business. Oftentimes, the rewards for these competitions include mentoring and cash prizes. Another popular way to get the necessary funds will be to investigate crowdfunding to source your idea. You can set up a Kickstarter or a GoFundMe account explaining what your business is, what you have done so far, and how the money you raise will help you move forward. Crowdfunding is very popular, so you have to make sure that your pitch is convincing enough to cut through the noise. You also want to make sure that the reasons are worthy of people giving you money.

The Ugly Truth

Initially, you probably won't make much money. The first couple of months might not be profitable. However, if you can survive these first few months and begin to turn a profit, then you will be okay. You want to keep detailed notes of your business sales and what you are making. For example, you can use an Excel spreadsheet to track your business expenses. Break down what everything will cost from shipping to what it costs to have your products manufactured to the packaging to the money you spent on advertisements. Keep it in a list.

Then keep a daily count of how many sales you are making and what the orders are. That way you can see what products are most popular and reinvest in those products. You can also see if certain products are not making you any money.

If you see that you need to cut costs, do not be afraid to do so. Do you really need to have that branded potpourri patch when people open your package? Try to be as lean or spend as less as possible, then you can upgrade the experience as you go. Try to make it out the first month so you can really start seeing a profit from what your orders are. Again, always reinvest your money back into the business and do things that work. So many people lose their business because they take too much money out.

If you see that you are not making as much money as you want initially, do not give up. Keep going. However, if you are burning through thousands of dollars every month, you may need to come up with a different strategy. And of course, everyone needs to have a point where they say I need to pivot before totally turning in the towel. Determine what the throwing in the towel moment is for you. The most important thing is if something isn't working, learn from it and if you keep doing that you will find the winning strategy.

Other Things To Keep In Mind

As a business owner, keep all your receipts for tax purposes. If you are going out to eat and discussing business, keep the receipt. Buying equipment for your business is another business expense. Services costs that you pay freelancers are also business expenses and can be used as a tax write-off. Other expenses you need to keep records of include electricity and internet, especially if you are working from a home office. Keep track of your cell phone bill or any expenses related to your business. Have the receipts and make sure you talk to your accountant. Having a good accountant is also ideal because if you are making over $10,000 every quarter, you will need to pay taxes. When you speak to your accountant, they will let you know the best way to make those payments. It sucks for you to have a lot of money, and then have to give that money up because of taxes. Stay on top of your tax obligations.

You also want to consider ways that you can save your money. Just because you have your own business does not mean that you can save your money. Your account will be able to position the best ways for you to save money and what accounts you can use as a self-employed person. One of the most popular ways to save money is to use a solo 401(K). This type of savings plan allows you to save up to $50,000 a year. You will also want to try to look into affordable medical costs. You can check out the Freelancers Union for some of the best medical insurance policies for self-employed people and business owners.

At some point, you will want to consider outsourcing tasks that are not making you a lot of money. Some entrepreneurs spend so much time doing everything that they are not focusing on the tasks that bring in the most money. In this case, you will want to hire a virtual assistant to take care of tasks that you do not have time for or tasks that you do not enjoy doing. Fiverr is an excellent place to find low-cost virtual assistance. You can also Google virtual assistants from the Philippines or India for a low-cost virtual assistant that can help you with what you want to do. When you have located a virtual assistant that you may want to work with, you want to communicate with them to see how you guys communicate. Then you will give them an initial task to see how they handle it. Once they handle according to your liking and you hire them for a book of hours, you can use an app like Slack or WhatsApp to communicate with them and make sure they are helping you with what you need. A virtual assistant will free up a lot of time for you. That way you can spend your time on more important things like making designs for your business, sending emails, and working on advertisements.

Overall, be smart and grow your business. Your clothing business can succeed as long as you put the work into it. As you start to turn a profit, you can even craft your life to make sure that you are not letting your business consume you. Yes, you can have a business. Yes, you can have fun doing it, yes you can live your dreams. A business needs constant investment like a tree needs constant water. You have all the tools you need. Now get to watering

CONCLUSION

Thank for making it through to the end of How to Start a Clothing Company: Learn Branding, Business, Outsourcing, Graphic Design, Fabric, Fashion Line Apparel, Shopify, Fashion, Social Media and Instagram Marketing Strategy, let's hope it was informative and able to provide you with all of the tools you need to achieve your goals whatever they may be. There are a lot of different ways for you to get started and it is our goal to give you option so you can pick out the best one that works for you.

As a brief recap, in chapter 1 how to get your seller's permit, wholesale permit and setting up your business structure was discussed. Chapter 2 was a quick intro to branding. It is definitely not as difficult as people make it. Chapter 3 discussed different options you can use to bring your clothes to life. Chapter 4 is a glossary of basic fashion terms that you will need to know. Cut and sew designing and graphic designing where the subjects of Chapter 5, whereas in Chapter 6, the best ways to get your website up and running was discussed. In chapter 7, the types of manufacturers you can use were given in detail. In chapter 8, attention was brought to your Instagram marketing strategy and other marketing strategies. Chapter 9 walked you through order fulfillment and the book ends with chapter 10 which discusses the truth about the money you will see in your business.

Now the ball is in your court. You can start with one of the easiest steps which are to get your EIN number which can be done in a matter of minutes. Then take the next easiest step and then the next easiest step. Just act. Do not suffer from analysis paralysis. The action is the key to making your business work. There is only so much research you can do.

Jim Rohn once said, "Time is more valuable than money. You can get more money, but you cannot get more time." This book has outlined everything you needed to know to get started with your clothing company. Do not waste any more time. Just think. If you start today that can be the difference between you making a profit a year from now versus still waiting for the perfect time to start. Do not be thumb twiddler. Get to work.